INEKE FAES
& PATRICK
VAN
ROSENDAAL

BE

FOR KIDS OF ALL AGES
WITH INEKE FAES
& PATRICK VAN ROSENDAAL

LANNOO

NY.

FAMILY

FOREWORD

How often do you move to another city and immediately meet its most famous Belgian, who knows every corner of New York City and turns out to be an incredibly nice guy? The answer, of course, is never. But that's what happened to me during my very first days in The Big Apple.

This is Patrick van Rosendaal's third 'BE NY' book, written jointly with his charming wife, Ineke Faes. It is a positive, funny, and useful book that leaves out none of the information you need to know when visiting. Of course, there are the 'must-sees' and 'must-dos', but what makes this BE NY Family really special are the tiny things you will never learn anywhere else, such as facts about dog names and toilet paper. It is a page-turner and it also caters to kids, offering details on where to find the best hot dogs or where to rent bicycles of all sizes. And so much more ... Rest assured that you will have your best visit ever to New York City when you tour with Patrick and his team of city guides.

Enjoy the book, take it everywhere with you but, first and foremost: enjoy this magnificent city, to which Patrick and Ineke, like so many others, have lost their hearts.

Cathy Buggenhout
Consul General of Belgium

New York: One big playground

WHY THIS BOOK?

Many people leave their children behind with grandma and grandpa when they go on a city trip to New York, or they wait until the kids are 18 before going together to discover the city. Which is a shame, because if there's one city that has a lot to offer to kids, it's New York. All the museums have attractions for children and youths, it's very common to bring children along to a restaurant and if, as an adult, you're so impressed with those skyscrapers, just think how a child would react. And of course there are all the amazing merry-go-rounds in New York, the tranquility of Central Park, the High Line in the heart of the city, the fantastic playgrounds and toy shops and all the cruises you could take. Actually, New York is one big playground. For adults yes, but definitely for children too.

FUN FACT
More than 8.6 million people live in New York, almost 2 million of whom are under the age of 18.

FUN FACT
The Brooklyn Children's Museum was the first museum in the world created especially for children.

WHO IS PATRICK VAN ROSENDAAL?

How he lost his heart to New York, how he sometimes had to struggle to survive and how he finally obtained his much-coveted American citizenship: you can read all about it in BE NY: *From Tourist to New Yorker*. Since its publication, Patrick's life has shifted into high gear. From one of the many tour guides in the city, he has become the city guide for Belgian and Dutch visitors to New York, recognizable by his canary-yellow jacket. Patrick is a pedigree storyteller. He can bombard you with facts and figures but he can also surprise you with original stories and juicy anecdotes or show you places you never would have found without a guide.

He got to know Ineke when she was travelling in New York and it didn't take much convincing to get her to move to The Big Apple. Their daughter Marie was born there and she has helped Patrick see New York in a different light.

Patrick has lived in Paris and London, he studied at the Vlerick Business School and, before moving to New York, he worked as a sales and marketing manager.

WHO IS INEKE FAES?

Ineke met Patrick at a rooftop bar with a view of the Manhattan skyline. It was love at first sight and Ineke didn't think twice before leaving everything behind and moving to New York. Romantic comedies pale in comparison.

A year later Marie was born, a very sociable, active and curious little girl. Marie discovered the city together with Patrick and Ineke. Ineke started writing the BE NY blog, where she shares cool spots and new places that are interesting for parents with children. This book is the obvious next step.

The daughter of an instrument maker and a graphic designer, Ineke grew up with music and art. She has taken classes in piano, cello, drawing and yoga and taught for more than six years in a creative primary school in Antwerp.

—

FACEBOOK.COM/BENYFAMILY
WWW.BENY.BE/BLOG
INSTAGRAM/PATRICKVANROSENDAAL

STROLLING AROUND (0-3 YEARS)

WALK: HOW ABOUT FROM NORTH TO SOUTH?

24 - 61

ELLIOT 39
Sleeping in the city that never sleeps
Toy stores in New York
New York baby

MAX 47
The little cover boy
Take me a picture
Mommy/daddy and me classes
Date night

MARKUS 53
King of Queens
Hacks: inexpensive New York
Picnic parks

TODDLING AROUND (3-6 YEARS)

WALK: ONLY THE BEST FROM UPPER EAST TO UPPER WEST

62 - 91

MARIE 73
A bubble of happiness
New York City or Museum City?
On the merry-go-round

BLUE 81
My something blue
Will you marry me?
NY-style pizza

LILY AND EVIE 87
Famous twins
Movie time
Unicorn is the new black

ROLLING AROUND
(6-9 YEARS)

JUMPING AROUND
(9-12 YEARS)

DRIVING AROUND
(12-21 YEARS)

New York in a nutshell

GEOGRAPHY

There are 50 states within the United States, one of which is New York. There are many cities in New York State but, if you're holding this book, you're probably planning a visit to New York City.

Think New York and you probably think Manhattan high-rise. But the city is much bigger, of course. New York consists of five large areas or boroughs: Manhattan, The Bronx in the north, Queens in the east, Brooklyn in the southeast and, finally, Staten Island in the south.

Each borough has its own neighborhoods; Manhattan's being the most famous.

Their names are generally of ethnic or geographical origin. The former would include Chinatown, Koreatown and Little Italy. The latter includes Upper East Side, Upper West Side, the West Village, Lower East Side, SoHo (South of Houston), NoHo (North of Houston), TriBeCa (Triangle Below Canal Street), NoLIta (North of Little Italy), FiDi (Financial District), DUMBO (Down Under Manhattan and Brooklyn Bridge Overpass) and so on.

ORIENTATION

Manhattan, with the exception of Lower Manhattan, is crisscrossed by its well-known grid of streets and avenues. This makes finding your way a piece of cake. Follow these guidelines and you'll have a hard time getting lost:

- Avenues run from north to south. Streets from east to west.
- If you're heading north they call that Uptown, if you're heading south it's Downtown.
- 5th Avenue divides Manhattan into east and west. When you see the letters E or W in front of a street name (for example, E 50th Street), that tells you on which side of 5th Avenue your destination is located.
- The majority of streets are one-way; even-numbered streets run eastwards. So by looking at the traffic you can tell in which direction to head.
- The distance between streets is usually around 260 ft. The distance between avenues is about three or four times that.
- New Yorkers count in blocks, so addresses are specified by them. For example, '56th Street between 5th and 6th'.

A tip from Patrick

Watch out for the avenues in the Midtown and Upper Manhattan region. Avenues are numbered from east to west and from 1 to 12 but, in a large area of Manhattan, after 1st, 2nd and 3rd you get Lexington, Madison and Park Avenue, and only then 5th, 6th, 7th, etc.

HOW DO YOU TRAVEL?

The predominant mode of transportation in New York is walking. 10 miles a day is not exceptional. For longer distances, take the subway, but if you're looking to get from A to B in comfort, you could always take a cab. Only a nutcase would actually try to explore Manhattan in a rental car.

FUN FACT
The winter of 1780 was so harsh that New York Harbor froze and you could walk on the ice from Manhattan to Staten Island.

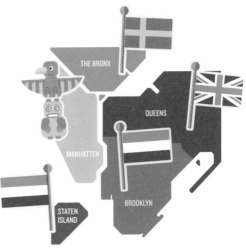

HOW DID THE BOROUGHS GET THEIR NAMES?

Manhattan comes from the Algonquin Lenape Indians, the native inhabitants of the island. They called Manhattan 'Manahatta', which means something like hilly island.

Queens was one of the twelve New York counties under British rule and owes its name to Queen Catherine of Braganza, wife of King Charles II of England.

Brooklyn is derived from Breukelen, a town in the Netherlands. It is a reminder of the time when New York was still under Dutch rule, when its name was still New Amsterdam.

The same goes for Staten Island. *Staaten Eylandt* was a Dutch trading post and refers to the *Staten-Generaal* (The States-General), the Dutch parliament.

The Bronx is named after the Swede Jonas Bronck, the European pioneer who settled there and who amassed a considerable amount of land.

Ready, set, go!

Get ready for a fantastic journey. Before you go, prepare yourself a bit by leafing through this book. That way, you could learn something about New York in advance and show your family around just like a real guide. Make sure to check the calendar (page 17) for special events during your stay in New York. Holidays, parades, film festivals; you don't need to miss a thing.

A tip from Marie

Take some toys with you on the trip. Triangular pencils or chalk are convenient when travelling because they don't roll off the table.

A tip from Patrick

This isn't a city trip but a world journey. Don't forget your passport and make sure your debit and credit cards are accepted in the United States.

A tip from Ineke

Before you set out on your trip, you should apply online for ESTA (Electronic System for Travel Authorization) or you won't be allowed into the US. If need be, you can use one of the terminals at the airport. (esta.cbp.dhs.gov/esta)

Hotels

Most hotels are child-friendly and have enough cribs or high chairs available, although it can't hurt to inquire in advance.

There are so many hotels in New York, there's plenty of choice. Here are a few to get you started:

BELVEDERE
319 W 48th St., Midtown
www.belvederehotelnyc.com
Centrally located at Times Square and budget-friendly. Walking distance from the M&M's Store.

TRYP BY WINDHAM TIMES SQUARE
345 W 35th St., Midtown
www.tryptimessquaresouth.com
Centrally located, close to the busy and perpetually buzzing Times Square and easily reachable by subway. There are rooms with bunk beds and in-room gaming is also possible.

PARKER NEW YORK
119 W 56th St., Midtown
www.parkernewyork.com
This chic hotel is two blocks from Central Park. It has a 'secret' burger restaurant, a magnificent indoor pool on the roof with a view of Central Park, and a junior suite that has plenty of room for a family of four or five.

CROSBY STREET HOTEL
79 Crosby St., SoHo
www.firmdalehotels.com
This luxurious boutique hotel is very trendy and also perfect for a stay with older children. Dogs are welcome too. It's located between Tompkins and Washington Square Parks, ideal parks for a morning stroll, with or without a dog. The hip SoHo district is nearby too.

WI-FI IN NY

Not only do all the cafes and restaurants have Wi-Fi, you can also access the internet on the subway. In T-Mobile phone stores you can buy an unlimited weekly pass for $30. Phone booths have disappeared from the streets and have been replaced by Wi-Fi masts. There are 7,500 spread throughout the city. If you're close to one you can easily access the internet.

USEFUL APPS

Google Maps: for easily mapping out your route.
NYC Subway: an offline subway map.
Yelp: want to know whether the beauty shop next to your hotel is worthwhile? Check it on Yelp.
Uber: for families with small children, UberFAMILY is the way to go. From 12 months, 22 lbs and 31 inches you can use the IMMI Go car seat. Don't forget to reserve it through the app (it costs $10 extra). The Car Seat Lady has a helpful YouTube film: 'How to buckle a child in the IMMI Go car seat.'

HOW DO YOU GET FROM JFK AIRPORT TO MANHATTAN?

There are several ways to get to your hotel from JFK. It all depends on your budget and your penchant for adventure. After a long flight you deserve to get to your hotel as quickly as possible; one of the reasons Uber's popularity is booming. If your budget dictates, you could share a car. Prefer going in Jay-Z style? Opt for the luxury SUV.

PUBLIC TRANSPORTATION

Depending on the airport, you can easily get to Manhattan either on the subway (JFK) or by train (Newark). Very trustworthy, no traffic jams and the cheapest option. A ticket for the *airtrain* from JFK can be bought only after transferring at Jamaica station, where you can also buy a ticket for the second half of your journey.

A tip from Patrick

Don't let yourself be talked into taking a cheap shuttle bus from the airport. Inexpensive, yes, but do you really want to stop at every hotel, packed like sardines, only to arrive at your hotel completely exhausted after an endless journey?

SUBWAY TIPS

The subway is the best and cheapest way to travel. A ticket costs $2.75. You can buy refillable cards with cash or credit card from the large vending machines on the platforms. Instead of a PIN code, you need to enter a five-digit zip code. Let your imagination run wild: as long as there are five digits, anything's okay.

You can use a card for up to four people. If you're staying for a week, an unlimited Metrocard ($32) may be worthwhile. A card for 30 days costs $121. Unlimited cards are non-transferable, of course.

Make sure you're on the right side of the platform, uptown or downtown. That could save you a lot of back and forth. You can check for delays or work in progress on www.mta.info.

JETLAG STRESS

West is best:

After arriving, it's best to stay awake as long as possible. That'll get you into the right rhythm as quickly as possible. Up early? No problem! The Apple Store on 5th Avenue is open day and night, all year round. Or you could go for breakfast at a 24-hour diner or walk around and see the city wake up.

East is a beast:

If you've visited America from Europe, it's recommended that you take a 3-hour nap when you get back home and then return to your normal rhythm. Most people find travelling eastwards more tiring than travelling westwards.

TIPS FOR NOT LOSING YOUR CHILD

The Plaza Hotel is where Kevin McCallister from *Home Alone 2* ends up after losing his parents at the airport and winding up alone in New York. Would you rather avoid this scenario because you don't expect your kid to be as independent as Kevin McCallister (Macaulay Culkin)?

Here are a few tips:

1. An ID wristband with Mom and Dad's phone number.
2. A non-permanent tattoo of phone numbers on your child's hand. This is what we use with Marie. Available at www.safetytat.com
3. Hadn't thought about it in advance and already in New York? Don't worry! Write your number on their arm with eyeliner. Fix it with some hairspray and it's guaranteed to stay on all day. (Tip: don't forget the country code.)
4. Give clear instructions. Make sure your kids know they have to get off at the very next subway station in case they don't manage to get out of the car on time. Have them wait against a wall while you take the next train to that station. Looking for them above ground isn't such a good idea because you just disappear into the crowd. An anxious child should approach a policeman or a mother with children.
5. Dressing your children in the conspicuous yellow BE NY colors is also an option.

A tip from Patrick

Looking for more tips and new places to discover? Check out the 'BE NY Minute' YouTube channel.

▶ YOUTUBE.COM/BENYMINUTE

12 Months in New York

Ice cream for breakfast? Barbecue on the street? On the subway in your underpants? It's all possible in New York! Make sure to check the calendar because every month is chock full of things to do.

JANUARY

January 1: New Year's Day

January 6:
Epiphany/Three Kings' Day
Parade with camels on Upper East Side, puppets and, of course, the three kings, Caspar, Melchior and Balthazar.
(www.elmuseo.org)

2nd Sunday:
No Pants Subway Ride
On this day, hundreds of people take the subway dressed only in their underpants. Groups of scantily clad New Yorkers coming from different locations gather in Union Square.
(www.improveverywhere.com)

3rd Monday:
Martin Luther King Jr. Day
A holiday in honor of Martin Luther King Jr., who fought for civil rights. Many shops are closed.

January or February:
Chinese New Year
Go to the Lunar New Year Parade in Chinatown where there is also a festival.

FEBRUARY

1st Saturday (or other February days with snow):
Ice Cream for Breakfast Day

A tip from Marie

Milk and Cream Cereal Bar (159 Mott Street, NoLIta) where they mix ice cream with cereal.

February 9: Bagel Day
(see page 193 for the tastiest bagels)

February 14: Valentine's Day
Take a picture at the Love Sculpture on 6th Ave. at 55th St.

3rd Monday: Presidents' Day
This holiday, originally in honor of George Washington, who was born on February 22, is now a celebration of the incumbent and all former presidents.

End of February-beginning of March: International Children's Film Festival (www.nyicff.org)

MARCH

March 17:
St. Patrick's Day
The biggest parade in the world is in New York. It is held on March 17 unless it's a Sunday, in which case it takes place on the preceding Saturday.

March 29:
Patrick van Rosendaal's birthday
I hope those participating in today's tour have brought a present ;-)

End of March-beginning of April: Macy's Flower Show
Macy's welcomes the spring with an amazing floral exhibition.
(151 W 34th Street, Midtown)

APRIL

Easter
Join one of the many egg hunts or the Easter Parade on 5th Avenue between 49th and 57th Streets, where everybody tries to outdo everyone else with the most eccentric hats.

April 22: Earth Day
From car-free streets to activities in museums aimed at raising awareness about our planet's future. The activities differ from year to year so check online to see what's happening.

April 26: Pretzel Day
No question that you have to buy a pretzel on the street today, just like all New Yorkers do.

Second half of April: Tribeca Film Festival
(www.tribecafilm.com)

End of April: Sakura Matsuri Cherry Blossom Festival
Enjoy the beautiful cherry blossoms in Brooklyn Botanical Garden.
(www.bbg.org)

FUN FACT
Together, we spend 1.9 billion dollars on chocolate and candy for Easter, putting this holiday in second place, after Halloween, of course.

MAY

1st Sunday in May: Five Boro Bike Tour
A bike tour through the city's five neighborhoods. The proceeds go to providing cycling lessons for adults and children.
(www.bike.nyc)

FUN FACT
Until after World War II, anyone who wanted to move had to do it at the same time, on May 1, better known as 'Moving Day.'

May 6: No Diet Day
On this day there's no dieting, one of New Yorkers' biggest hobbies. Since you're not counting calories anyway, why not go for a burger with fries and a crazy shake at Black Tap? That'll certainly take care of you for a year.

Around May 29 and July 11: Manhattanhenge
(see page 56)

Last Monday of May: Memorial Day
This coincides with Fleet Week. Visit (for free) one of the many marine ships docking at the New York Passenger Ship Terminal on the Hudson River on the west side of Manhattan.

JUNE

Beginning of June: Governors Ball
Three-day music festival.
(www.govisland.com)

Beginning of June: Big Apple Barbecue Block Party
The biggest culinary festival in America, dedicated to the barbecue.
(www.bigapplebbq.org)

First Friday in June:
National Donut Day
An important day in New York. Important enough to set your alarm clock for: if you oversleep, all the donuts will be gone.

Middle of June:
Egg Rolls, Egg Creams & Empanadas Festival
Proof that New York really is a cultural melting pot. Look forward to Jewish, Chinese and Puerto Rican delicacies and music.

Middle or end of June:
Mermaid Parade
(see page 125)

Last Sunday of June:
Lesbian and Gay
Pride Day Parade

(see page 125)

In New York, same-sex couples have been allowed to get married since July 24, 2011. In 2001 the Netherlands became the first country where this was enacted; Belgium was second, in 2003.

SUMMERTIME

Shakespeare in the park in the Delacorte Theater in Central Park
(www.publictheater.org)

Philharmonic in the Park Concerts
(www.nyphil.org)

Bryant Park Summer Film Festival
(www.bryantpark.org)

Summer Stage
(www.summerstage.org)

Smorgasburg food market
(www.smorgasburg.com)

JULY

July 4:
Independence Day
The United States were declared no longer a part of the British Empire on July 4, 1776.
Look for the best place to watch the fireworks. It's always amazing! Each year there's a Hot Dog Eating Contest on Coney Island.
(see page 126)

(see page 126)

Beginning of July:
Hudson Valley Balloon Festival
(www.dcrcoc.org/balloonfestival)

3rd Wednesday in July:
National Hot Dog Day

3rd Sunday in July:
National Ice Cream Day

An estimated 150 million hot dogs are consumed on Independence Day.

AUGUST

End of July-beginning of August:
Lincoln Center Out of Doors
Outdoor parties and free open-air concerts.
(www.lincolncenter.org)

Late August - early September
US Open Tennis Championships

In 1902, Willis Carrier invented the first modern air conditioner. Thank you, Willis!

SEPTEMBER

1st Monday in September:
Labor Day
Celebrated since 1894. In Europe it's celebrated on May 1.

Middle of September:
Feast of San Gennaro
Street festival in Little Italy.

September 29:
Coffee Day

OCTOBER

National Pizza Month
(see page 85)

2nd Monday in October:
Columbus Day
Celebrating the day Christopher Columbus landed in the Americas October 12, 1492. There's a large statue of Columbus in the center of Columbus Circle.

End of October:
Halloween Dog Parade
Maybe even better than Halloween: dogs in costume with their dressed up owners in Tompkins Square Park.
(www.tompkinssquaredogrun.com/halloween)

October 31:
Halloween
Every year there's a magnificent parade in The Village around Washington Square Park. Many neighborhoods hold their own small parades.

NOVEMBER

1st Sunday in November:
Marathon through the five boroughs
(www.tcsnycmarathon.org)

Beginning of November:
New York Comedy Festival
(nycomedyfestival.com)

November 11:
Veterans' Day
Dedicated to American military veterans of all wars.

Last Wednesday in November:
Balloon inflation around the Museum of National History
The giant balloons (easily 50 ft high and 65 ft wide) for Macy's Thanksgiving Day Parade are inflated on this day.
(Upper West Side)

4th Thursday in November:
Thanksgiving
Macy's Thanksgiving Day Parade from the Museum of Natural History to Macy's.
(34th St. and Broadway)

Friday after Thanksgiving:
Black Friday
Mega-discounts everywhere. Expect long lines, especially at Macy's.

Wednesday after Thanksgiving:
Rockefeller Center Christmas Tree Lighting
www.rockefellercenter.com

WINTER

Visit the real Santa at Macy's
(November to December)

Charming Christmas markets: Union Square Holiday Market (59th St. and Central Park West), Winter Village in Bryant Park and the Holiday Fair in Grand Central.

Also worthwhile:
Holiday Train Shows
During the Christmas season, miniature trains ride around in Brooklyn Botanical Garden and in Grand Central.

Christmas show:
The Rockettes in Radio City Music Hall
Lithe dancers give you their best. Kitschy, but typically New York.
(from October to December)

DECEMBER

Hanukah
The Jewish community celebrates Hanukah in Manhattan, including lighting the world's largest menorah, a nine-branched candleholder.
(W 59th Street and 5th Ave)

December 24: Christmas Eve
December 25: Christmas Day
December 31: New Year's Eve
All over the world people watch the 'Ball Drop' in Times Square on TV.

FuN FACT
If you want to go to Times Square to watch, take a diaper or incontinence pants. Because if you've got your hands on a good spot and you need to go to the toilet, it won't be yours anymore when you get back.

A tip from Ineke
You can find a bunch of activities on New York's official website under 'events.'
www.nyc.gov

'HOW DO YOU GET THERE?'

NEW YORKERS ARE ALWAYS BUSY AND ON THE MOVE. SO WHICH MODE OF
TRANSPORTATION DO THEY PREFER? A YELLOW CAB, THE FERRY, A HORSE AND
CARRIAGE OR MAYBE A HELICOPTER? MOST NEW YORKERS JUST GO ON FOOT, BY
SUBWAY OR THEY TAKE AN UBER TAXI.

MOST NEW YORKERS DON'T OWN A CAR.
NEW YORKERS WALK MORE THAN ANY OTHER RESIDENTS OF THE UNITED STATES.
EVERY DAY ABOUT 5.6 MILLION PEOPLE TAKE THE SUBWAY.
THERE ARE 13,587 YELLOW CABS IN THE CITY.
THERE ARE MORE THAN 60,000 BLACK CARS, 46,000 OF WHICH WORK FOR UBER.

8.4 MILLION INHABITANTS

5.6 MILLION PEOPLE
TAKE THE SUBWAY

46,000 UBER
VEHICLES

13,587 YELLOW
CABS

STROLLING AROUND

HOW ABOUT FROM NORTH TO SOUTH?

(0-3 YEARS)

STROLLING AROUND

0-3 YEARS **+/- 5 MILES**

MIDTOWN – CHELSEA – MEATPACKING
DISTRICT – WESTVILLAGE – TRIBECA –
FINANCIAL DISTRICT

<u>PART I: NORTH</u>

1. SUBWAY STOP HUDSON YARDS
2. VESSEL
3. HUDSON PARK PLAYGROUND
4. HIGH LINE START POINT
5. NORTH RIVER LOBSTER COMPANY
6. INTREPID SEA, AIR & SPACE MUSEUM
7. CIRCLE LINE SIGHTSEEING CRUISES
8. ZAHA HADID
9. THE McKITTRICK HOTEL
10. HOTEL AMERICANO
11. AVENUES: THE WORLD SCHOOL
12. EMPIRE DINER
13. PIER 62 CAROUSEL
14. DAVID ZWIRNER
15. WOMEN'S JAIL
16. IAC
17. CHELSEA MARKET
18. THE STANDARD, HIGH LINE
19. WHITNEY MUSEUM OF AMERICAN ART
20. GANSEVOORT MARKET

SEE NEXT PAGE → → →

STROLLING AROUND

0-3 YEARS   **+/- 5 MILES**

MIDTOWN – CHELSEA – MEATPACKING DISTRICT – WESTVILLAGE – TRIBECA – FINANCIAL DISTRICT

PART 2: SOUTH

1 CHRISTIAN LOUBOUTIN
2 D'AGOSTINO
3 TEICH TOYS & BOOKS
4 BLEECKER PLAYGROUND
5 MAGNOLIA BAKERY
6 CARRIE BRADSHAY'S APARTMENT
7 VILLAGE APOTHECARY
8 EMPLOYEES ONLY
9 FRIENDS APARTMENT
10 CHALAIT
11 CHILDREN'S MUSEUM OF THE ARTS
12 NEW YORK CITY FIRE MUSEUM
13 TRAPEZE SCHOOL NEW YORK – PIER 40
14 SPRING STREET SALT SHED
15 PIER 34 - VENTILATION HOLLAND TUNNEL
16 HI SPY VIEWING MACHINE
17 CITY VINEYARD
18 PIER 25
19 GRAND BANKS
20 TRIBECA SKATE PARK
21 THE REAL WORLD
22 TEARDROP PARK
23 IRISH HUNGER MEMORIAL
24 9/II MEMORIAL

Manhattan is more extensive than you may expect. From the completely new Hudson Yards district we descend via the High Line, museums and playgrounds towards Midtown. You can get something to eat at the former cookie factory in Meatpacking, buy a cupcake in West Village like Carrie Bradshaw or Chandler Bing, or relax on the Hudson. We end at the 9/11 Memorial, an impressive monument to the victims of the terrorist attacks etched in every New Yorker's memory. Since 2001, a new generation of youngsters has grown up, whose knowledge of the attacks comes only from their parents' stories. For them, the playgrounds we come across are at least as important as the modern architecture. But all their scrambling will also help them climb the Vessel, New York's Eiffel Tower.

PART I: NORTH

❶ HUDSON YARDS SUBWAY STOP

W 34th St. and 11th Ave.

This brand-new subway stop has been named after the large-scale redevelopment program, still underway. Money talks, bull*** walks. Hudson Yards cost more than 20 billion dollars and is the largest development project since Rockefeller Center in the 1930s. It will include more than 4,000 residences, 100 shops, a big school, modern offices, and luxury hotels and restaurants. More than 23,000 construction workers have been involved in this mega-project.

❷ VESSEL

W 34th St. and 11th Ave.

www.hudsonyardsnewyork.com

The centerpiece of Hudson Yards and a new New York landmark, Vessel is a 150 ft high modern tower, which you may also climb. Good for your fitness, because with its 154 flights of stairs and 2,500 steps you'll be at it for a while. The New York Times called Vessel 'The $150 million stairway to nowhere'. Not short of ambitiousness, the aim is for Vessel to be as popular as the Eiffel Tower in Paris.

❸ HUDSON PARK PLAYGROUND

Hudson Yards Park, 542 W 36th St.

+1 212-239-1619

🕐 Mo.-Su. 7 a.m.-7 p.m.

This playground is ideal for letting the little ones clamber around for a while. Everything is brand-new and super safe. Slightly fewer steps than Vessel, but enough climbing equipment to get them in shape for the ultimate achievement.

❹ HIGH LINE START POINT

5861 High Line

www.thehighline.org

🕐 Open 24 hours

The High Line is a 1.45-mile-long park built on an elevated rail line that's no longer in use. It's not only a green vein running through the city, but also a route full of art. A whole slew of New Yorkers have received marriage proposals here, although it can be a risky business–many a ring has fallen through the small cracks. So watch out with those shaky hands.

⑤ NORTH RIVER LOBSTER COMPANY

12th Ave. and W 41st St.
www.northriverlobsterco.com
+1 212-630-8831
🕐 Mo.-Th. 9 a.m.-5:30 p.m.,
Fr.-Su. 10 a.m.-6:30 p.m.

A cruise on the Hudson while enjoying fresh lobster *and* a view of the New York skyline? At the North River Lobster Company it's possible, even without a seven-digit account balance.

⑥ INTREPID SEA, AIR & SPACE MUSEUM

Pier 86, W 46th St. and 12th Ave.
www.intrepidmuseum.org
+1 212-245-0072
🕐 Mo.-Su. 10 a.m.-5 p.m.

Visiting an aircraft carrier–it's many a young (and older) child's dream. But Intrepid is much more than that. How about a visit to a space shuttle or a top-secret submarine? Good news for those unable to tear their children away: you can stay overnight. Or convince your offspring to come along to the science playground on Pier 84. The water pumps and miniature canals with sluices are always a big hit.

⑦ CIRCLE LINE SIGHTSEEING CRUISES

Pier 83, W 42nd St.
www.circleline.com
+1 212-563-3200
🕐 Mo.-Su. 9 a.m.-7 p.m.

Legs aching from all the walking but still wanting to see more of New York? In that case a Circle Line Sightseeing Cruise is a good idea. The professional guides provide you with interesting details about the city while you sail around Manhattan Island in three hours.

⑧ ZAHA HADID

520 W 28th St.

This futuristic apartment building was designed by Zaha Hadid's architecture firm and is an impressive sight. A pied-à-terre next to the upper crust will easily set you back a cool $5 million.

⑨ THE McKITTRICK HOTEL

530 W 27th St.
www.mckittrickhotel.com
+1 212-904-1883

Ever heard of 'Sleep No More?' You can watch the modern version of Shakespeare's 'Macbeth' here. For three hours, you wander through an abandoned hotel where all kinds of things are going on everywhere. You will be immersed in different ambiances with accompanying music and find yourself lured into a multitude of deep mysteries.

⑩ HOTEL AMERICANO

518 W 27th St.
www.hotel-americano.com
+1 212-216-0000

The rooftop bar of this amazing hotel is where I met Ineke. I'm therefore a bit biased but I still think this is the ideal location to make a deep impression on your (future) partner.

⑪ AVENUES: THE WORLD SCHOOL

259 10th Ave.
www.avenues.org

This school has the reputation of being one of the best, if not the best in New York. Ineke and I would love to send Marie there but with tuition at more than $50,000 a year, we'll just have to keep on dreaming.

⑫ EMPIRE DINER

210 10th Ave.
www.empire-diner.com
+1 212-355-2277
🕐 Mo.-Su. 8 a.m.-1 a.m.

This magnificent diner combines New York tradition – the iconic structure was built in 1976 – with a modern interior and delicious dishes. Not surprising that so many pictures are taken here.

⑬ PIER 62 CAROUSEL

Cross over on 22nd St.,
from Pier 62, Chelsea
www.pier62carouselnyc.com

The Pier 62 Carousel consists of 33 hand-carved wooden animals, all found in Hudson River Valley, and a chariot. From a bear to a beaver or a turkey, all the animals are equally beautiful. The carousel is closed in the winter so before you go make sure to check online that it's open. Not far from there is the Chelsea Waterside Play Area. The water in this water playground comes at you from all angles, so get ready to be soaked.

⑭ DAVID ZWIRNER

537 W 20th St.
www.davidzwirner.com
+1 212-517-8677
🕐 Tu.-Sa. 10 a.m.-6 p.m.

Are you a fledgling art lover or a passionate collector? It doesn't matter. There are so many art galleries in Chelsea that there's something for everyone. David Zwirner is possibly the most renowned. He represents big names such as Marlene Dumas, Michaël Borremans, Luc Tuymans and Daniel Richter.

⑮ WOMEN'S JAIL

You wouldn't think it with all its art galleries, but until not so long ago this used to be one of the roughest neighborhoods in New York. The women's prison that was operational until 2012 is the last testimony to this. The prison was shut down permanently after Superstorm Sandy. The decorations on the front are proof that this brick building dating from 1931 once served as a guesthouse for seamen.

⑯ IAC

555 W 18th St.
www.iac.com
+1 212-314-7300

The IAC Building (InterActiveCorp, owner of hundreds of media and internet companies including Tinder) is the first building in New York to have been designed by the Canadian-American architect, Frank Gehry. It's particularly well known for its vaulted glass facade. *Vanity Fair* once called it one of the world's most attractive office buildings. When completed in 2007, the building's lobby featured the world's then-largest high-definition screen.

⑰ CHELSEA MARKET

75 9th Ave.
www.chelseamarket.com
+1 212-652-2110
🕐 Mo.-Sa. 7 a.m.-2 a.m., Su. 8 a.m-10 p.m.

Chelsea Market was once Nabisco's headquarters, home of the centenarian Oreo. Now it's a great place for browsing through shops and food stalls. Today's tidbit of trivia: this piece of New York history is now owned by Google.

⑱ THE STANDARD, HIGH LINE

848 Washington St.
www.standardhotels.com
+1 212-645-4646

The Standard Hotel is where I asked Ineke to marry me. In the morning I realized I was looking at my two great loves at once: Ineke woke up next to me while behind her the Manhattan skyline was bathing in the morning sunlight. Nine months later another love was added: Marie. We sometimes laughingly call her The Standard baby.

⑲ WHITNEY MUSEUM OF AMERICAN ART

99 Gansevoort St., Meatpacking District
www.whitney.org
+1 212-570-3600
🕐 Su.-Mo. 10:30 a.m.-6 p.m.,
Tu. closed, We.-Th. 10:30 a.m.-6 p.m.,
Fr.-Sa. 10:30 a.m.-10 p.m.

This museum displays American art from the 20th and 21st centuries. The permanent collection consists of more than 21,000 works of art, painted, photographed and filmed by more than 3000 artists. This new building does the art even more justice. New parents need not worry: there are organized stroller tours.

⑳ GANSEVOORT MARKET

353 W 14th St.
www.gansmarket.com
+1 646-678-3231
🕐 Mo.-Su. 8 a.m.-9 p.m.

Gansevoort Market used to be where New Yorkers came to buy their vegetables, meat and milk. Instead of screaming vendors, now you can see menus on flat screens. Don't miss Marie's favorite: Milk and Cream Cereal Bar, where they mix cereal with ice cream. The perfect recipe for a summer breakfast.

PART 2: SOUTH

① CHRISTIAN LOUBOUTIN

59 Horatio St.
www.us.christianlouboutin.com/us_en/
+1 212-255-1910
🕐 Mo.-Sa. 11 a.m.- 7 p.m., Su. noon-6 p.m.

Louboutin's shoes with their fire-engine red soles are in demand all over the world. This shop exudes total luxury. You don't see only women here, but also men who come to buy shoes as presents for their partners. For instance, as a push present, a present a father gives to the mother of their child after the birth. This tradition is growing in popularity in New York so the gift may be more than a mere silver charm.

② D'AGOSTINO

790 Greenwich St.
www.dagnyc.com
+1 212-691-9198
🕐 Mo.-Su. 7 a.m.-10 p.m.

This small supermarket chain has been run by the D'Agostino family since 1932. From organic vegetables to diapers, fruit or sushi, they have it all here.

③ TEICH TOYS & BOOKS

573 Hudson St., between Bank St. and West 11th St., West Village
www.teichtoys.com
+1 212-924-2232
🕐 Mo.-Sa. 9 a.m.-7 p.m., Su. 10 a.m.-6 p.m.

A toy shop you yourself would have designed. They have a life-size locomotive children can play in. Actually, the whole store looks like one great train that delivers all the toys you've ever dreamed of.

④ BLEECKER PLAYGROUND

Bleecker St. and W 11th St.
www.nycgovparks.org
+1 212-639-9675
🕐 Mo.-Su. 8 a.m.-8 p.m.

Just got done buying out Teich Toys & Books? Take your new toys right on over to Bleecker Playground, although you could easily enjoy yourself there even without any booty.

⑤ MAGNOLIA BAKERY

401 Bleecker St.
www.magnoliabakery.com
+1 212-462-2572
🕐 Su.-Th. 10 a.m.-10:30 p.m.,
Fr.-Sa. 10 a.m.-11:30 p.m.

This is the bakery where *Sex and the City* girlfriends, Carrie and Miranda, buy their cupcakes before eating them outside on a bench while discussing their love life. Feel free to do the same.

6 CARRIE BRADSHAW'S APARTMENT

64 Perry St.

From the cupcakes to the magnificent brownstone where Carrie Bradshaw lives in *Sex and the City*. It's easy to recognize the building by all the tourists taking pictures. Since word got out that Cynthia Nixon (Miranda Hobbes) is running for Governor of New York, the series has gained in popularity.

7 VILLAGE APOTHECARY

346 Bleecker St.
www.villageapothecary.com
+1 212-807-7566
🕐 Mo.-Fr. 8 a.m.-8 p.m., Sa. 9 a.m.-6 p.m., Su. 10 a.m.-5 p.m.

This pharmacy is one of the only small-scale independently-owned businesses in the neighborhood. When AIDS broke out in the 1980s, its doors remained open to everyone. For this and for their social commitment, they received a Proclamation from the Mayor's Office.

8 EMPLOYEES ONLY

510 Hudson St.
www.employeesonlynyc.com
+1 212-242-3021
🕐 Mo.-Su. 6 p.m.-4 a.m.

This hospitable speakeasy is well hidden behind a fortune teller's parlor. The bar has won several prizes, including some for the best cocktails. Those still around at 4 in the morning are offered a bowl of chicken soup. A magic remedy for a potential hangover.

9 FRIENDS APARTMENT

90 Bedford St.

Thirty-somethings still sharing an apartment? In New York this isn't out of the ordinary due to the extremely high prices. Not everyone is lucky enough to live in a rent-controlled apartment like the characters in *Friends*. Landlords of these residences are not allowed to raise rents indiscriminately. All other apartments hike their prices heftily every year. We also await our landlord's plans with some apprehension every year.

10 CHALAIT

299 W Houston St.
www.chalait.com
+1 646-922-8436
🕐 Mo.-Fr. 7 a.m.-6 p.m., Sa.-Su. 8 a.m.-5 p.m.

In the mood for an *avocado tartine* or a salmon and egg sandwich? Everything ordered here is served beautifully. The selection of matcha drinks is at least as extensive as the coffee menu, so my wife is a regular customer here.

11 CHILDREN'S MUSEUM OF THE ARTS

103 Charlton St.
www.cmany.org
+1 212-274-0986
🕐 Mo. noon-5 p.m., Tu.-We. closed, Th.-Fr. noon-6 p.m., Sa.-Su. 10 a.m.-5 p.m.

Fledgling artists can live it up here. Paint, clay, glue or slime? They have it all. The museum's name is misleading because the collection consists mostly of work created by young visitors from all over the world.

12 NEW YORK CITY FIRE MUSEUM

278 Spring St.
www.nycfiremuseum.org
+1 212-691-1303
🕐 Mo.-Su. 10 a.m.-5 p.m.

The New York City Fire Department has its own museum, which is specifically designed for children. From the bucket-brigades in Peter Stuyvesant's New Amsterdam to volunteer firemen and modern firefighting techniques; a visit to this museum is a journey through time.

⑬ TRAPEZE SCHOOL NEW YORK – PIER 40

www.trapezeschool.com
+1 212-242-8769

If the New York bustle gets too suffocating for you, why not stop for a lesson at the Trapeze School? You can glide upside down through the air with your hair flying in the wind. Anyone who dreams of a circus career can learn all the tricks of the trade here.

⑭ SPRING STREET SALT SHED

336 Spring St.

This depot for street salt is a magnified grain of salt made from concrete. Still, it's prettier than you'd expect. All the salt stored here, which usually comes from Chile or Argentina, is for keeping the streets of Manhattan snow-free during the winter snowstorms. The mountain of salt inside can reach as high as 65ft.

⑮ PIER 34 - VENTILATION HOLLAND TUNNEL

Hudson River Park
www.hudsonriverpark.org

What are those two towers doing in the water? They provide Holland Tunnel with fresh air. They can completely refresh the air in the tunnel in 90 seconds. The Holland Tunnel connects Manhattan with New Jersey

and its main asset is its amazing view of Manhattan.

⑯ HI SPY VIEWING MACHINE

These special binoculars bring New Jersey way up close for detailed viewing.

⑰ CITY VINEYARD

233 West St.
www.cityvineyardnyc.com
+1 646-677-8350
🕐 Mo.-Fr. 4 p.m.-10 p.m., Sa. 11 a.m.-10 p.m., Su. 11 a.m.-9 p.m.

Grab some food or a drink on this rooftop cafe on the waterfront while the grapes ripen next to you in the sun. So it's no big surprise that this place is so popular when the weather is good. Intimate concerts are also held here and, if the weather doesn't cooperate, there's always the covered patio.

⑱ PIER 25

West St. and N Moore St.
www.hudsonriverpark.org
🕐 Mo.-Su. 10 a.m.-10 p.m.

There's a playground at Pier 25 where you can keep cool in the summer thanks to the buckets that slowly fill and are then suddenly tipped upside down above you. There's also a mini golf course. It's well-kept, open all year and, above all, cheap ($6 a game). The awesome view of Freedom Tower is an added bonus.

⑲ GRAND BANKS

Pier 25
www.grandbanks.org
+1 212-660-6312
🕐 Mo.-Tu. 3 p.m.-midnight, We.-Fr. noon-midnight, Sa.-Su. 11 a.m.-midnight, winter: closed

This chic oyster bar on the deck of a historic fishing boat puts you in an ultimate vacation mood. Revel in the sunset with oysters, fresh fish and a glass of champagne. A bit on the decadent side but nonetheless attractive.

⑳ TRIBECA SKATE PARK

100 N Moore St.
www.hudsonriverpark.org
+1 212-627-2020
🕐 Mo.-Su. 8 a.m.-6 p.m.

An extensive skate park with a super-smooth track. Ideal for practicing tricks, for impressing your parents, or for scaring the living daylights out of them.

㉑ THE REAL WORLD

Rockefeller Park
www.tomostudio.com

The Real World looks like a playground but is actually a work of art by Tom Otterness. His fairytale bronzes of animals and people are a commentary on the financial world. Kids can't get enough of all these creatures great and small and the hundreds of pennies surrounding them.

㉒ TEARDROP PARK

Warren St. and Murray St.,
Battery Park City
www.bpcparks.org

This hidden playground has
a large slide, fun sprin-
klers and rocks to clamber
on. There's lots of shade
and you're completely
surrounded by green. The
chaotic, hectic metropolis
seems miles away. A prac-
tical tip: the toilets are on
the northwest side of the
Solaire Building.

㉓ IRISH HUNGER MEMORIAL

North End Ave. and Vesey St.
www.bpcparks.org
+1 212-267-9700
🕐 Mo.-Su. 11 a.m.-6:30 p.m.

An abandoned brick house,
brick walls, and a fallow
potato field. This is the
monument to the great
Irish famine of 1845-1850.
Artist Brian Tolle wishes
to demonstrate that, to
this day, hunger is often
due to limited access to
fertile land.

㉔ 9/11 MEMORIAL

180 Greenwich St.
www.911memorial.org
+1 212-312-8800
🕐 Mo.-Su. 7:30 a.m.-9 p.m.

The day the two hijacked
planes hit the Twin Towers
is etched in everyone's
memory. This monument is
a fine tribute to the victims
of the terrorist attacks.
The waterfalls symbolize
the New Yorkers' grief; the
new tower, higher than the
Twin Towers, is a sign that
the people of New York
will never give in to terror.
The museum contains all
you need to know about
the saddest day in New
York's recent history. The
Oculus station by architect
Santiago Calatrava puts the
finishing touch on this un-
intended makeover forced
on the city.

FUN FACT

Near the 9/11 Memorial is
the Survivor Tree, a tree that
survived the attacks.

FAVORITE SNACK: <u>MOM'S MILK</u>
LANGUAGES: <u>ENGLISH, DUTCH</u>
FAVORITE PARK: <u>CENTRAL PARK</u>
FAVORITE MODE OF TRANSPORTATION: <u>BABY CARRIER</u>
FAVORITE PLACE: <u>MARTHA'S COUNTRY BAKERY</u>
FAVORITE RESTAURANT: <u>ALL RESTAURANTS, EXCEPT THOSE WITH THREE MICHELIN STARS</u>
LIVES IN: <u>FOREST HILLS, QUEENS</u>

ELLIOT

A baby. Help! That's got to be the end of gourmet dining in starred restaurants. Nothing could be further from the truth. But I found this out by accident. As I did every week, after a tour I was ordering a Danish Dog at Claus Meyer in Grand Central Terminal when I saw that a new restaurant had opened next to it (Agern). I thought it would be a good idea to check it out with the wife and kid. We went in; I was dressed in shorts and my conspicuous yellow BE NY shirt. The attendants were very helpful, folding the stroller and placing Marie in a nicely designed high chair. Only once we had settled in did we see on the menu that we were in a Michelin starred restaurant... but it turned out OK. Kids are welcome everywhere. When we got the bill I was a bit less enthusiastic. Oh well, it gave me a story I could tell for years.

Nothing makes me happier than news from friends that they're going to have a baby. Because then I can share not only my knowledge as a guide but also what it's like to be a father in New York. When our friends Benoit and Nathalie told us that their family would be growing by one person, I couldn't resist immediately sharing all my tips and fun facts. But it's never too early to know.

In a city with 5.7 million subway passengers, 13,587 yellow cabs, more than 46,000 Uber taxis and numerous limos,

you'd think that transportation wouldn't be a problem but, believe me, when your bundle of joy is on the way you suddenly discover a whole lot of disadvantages. For instance, abrupt braking maneuvers, car seats (or, to be more precise, the lack thereof) and countless steps. Also, never tell a taxi driver why you're going to the hospital before you're sitting in the cab, or he'll refuse the ride because he's afraid of having a baby born on his back seat.

Until just a few years ago, there were no changing tables in men's toilets. With their petition on change.org, Ashton Kutcher and his wife Mila Kunis made sure that more and more men's restrooms are now equipped with baby changing tables. Our heroes! The acting couple has two children: daughter Wyatt and son Dimitri. So it may be that you find yourself in a restaurant, changing your baby's diaper next to Ashton Kutcher.

Since our first daughter turned out so well and now wanders cheerfully around the city, I'm starting to itch for a baby brother or sister for Marie. Especially after visiting Nathalie and Benoit to admire their little Elliot. Unfortunately we have to save some money first.

FUN FACT

Are you here for a four-day city trip? Every 4.4 minutes a new New Yorker is born. By the time you go home, the city will have grown by at least 1309 citizens.

A TIP FROM ELLIOT

MARTHA'S COUNTRY BAKERY

70-28 Austin St., Forest Hills, Queens
263 Bedford Ave., Williamsburg, Brooklyn
www.marthascountrybakery.com
+1 718-544-0088
Su.-Th. 6 a.m.-midnight, Fr.-Sa. 6 a.m.-1 a.m.

New York babies can sleep anywhere, preferably in a coffee house with some buzz in the background while mom and dad lick their fingers while enjoying delicious cakes. There's just one problem: choosing is a nightmare because the selection is so huge and everything is equally delicious.

 # A TIP FROM INEKE

WHITNEY MUSEUM OF AMERICAN ART

99 Gansevoort St., Meatpacking District
www.whitney.org
+1 212-570-3600
Su.-Mo. 10:30 a.m.-6 p.m., Tu. closed,
We.-Th. 10:30 a.m.-6 p.m., Fr.-Sa. 10:30 a.m.-10 p.m.

This museum regularly organizes stroller tours before opening its doors to the wider public. Is your little angel up early anyway? Turn your toddler into a little art expert. It's never too soon.

If you're visiting the museum with slightly older kids, you can create a new work of art together on weekends. Free guided tours for families are offered on Saturdays. On Fridays between 7 p.m. and 10 p.m. you can decide your own entrance fee.

TIPS FROM PATRICK

POTTERY BARN KIDS

1311 2nd Ave., between E 68th St. and E 69th St., Upper East Side
www.potterybarnkids.com
+1 212-879-4746
Mo.-Sa. 10 a.m.-7 p.m., Su. noon-6 p.m.

When Elliot was born we gave our new little friend a present of a Pottery Barn Kids towel embroidered with his name. You can personalize everything they sell here. Marie has a bunny-shaped knapsack with her name on it. When she wears it she's so cute we could eat her. Do you want a personalized present too? Then you're in luck: Pottery Barn has more than 90 stores worldwide.

BUILD-A-BEAR WORKSHOP

22 W 34th St.
www.buildabear.com
+1 212-863-4070
Mo.-Sa. 10 a.m.-9 p.m., Su. 11 a.m.-7 p.m.

Children can create their own little New Yorker here, shaped like a teddy bear, including a warm, beating heart. Want to guess what their favorite stuffed animal will be...?

FUN FACT

The term 'teddy bear' comes from President Theodore Roosevelt, whose nickname was Teddy. He was out hunting but refused to kill a bear that had been caught. This became the subject of a cartoon. Referring to the cartoon, a candy store owner who sold stuffed bears made by his wife called them Teddy's bear. And so the teddy bear was born.

FUN FACT

Gertrude Vanderbilt Whitney wished to donate 700 works of art to the Met (Metropolitan Museum of Art). The museum management refused. So she created her own museum: The Whitney Museum of American Art.

TOY STORES IN NEW YORK

It seems like the toy stores in New York are competing to see who can stock the most original toys. Looking for your baby's first camera or an eco-friendly play pizza your child can top? You can find it all here!

KIDDING AROUND
60 W 15th St., Flatiron District
+1 212-645-6337
Mo.-Sa. 10 a.m.-7 p.m.,
Su. 11 a.m.-6 p.m.
87 E 42nd St., Grand Central Terminal
+1 212-972-8697
Mo.-Fr. 8 a.m.-8 p.m., Sa. 10 a.m.-8 p.m., Su. 11 a.m.-6 p.m.
www.kiddingaroundtoys.com
In order to combat consumerism, New York parents increasingly prefer sustainable toys. Fortunately for us, Marie likes Plan Toys' recycled creations. We discovered these original toys in Kidding Around because, as a city guide, I like to go to Grand Central Terminal.

TEICH TOYS AND BOOKS
573 Hudson St., between Bank St. and West 11th St., West Village
www.teichtoys.com
+1 212-924-2232
Mo.-Sa. 9 a.m.-7 p.m.,
Su. 10 a.m.-6 p.m.
From knitted hot dogs to inventor's boxes or children's books about New York, this family business

is for New Yorkers and tourists alike. The store's big yellow toy locomotive is a child magnet.

ABC HOME FURNISHINGS
30 East 19th St.
www.abchome.com
+1 212-473-3000
Mo.-Sa. 10a.m.-7 p.m.,
Su. noon-6 p.m.
You wouldn't expect an interior design boutique to sell toys as well, but this one does. Marie can spend hours here just hugging all the teddy bears.

LEGO STORE
620 Fifth Ave. and E 50th St. next to Rockefeller Center, Midtown
200 Fifth Ave. and W 23rd St., Flatiron District
www.lego.com
Mo.-Su. 10 a.m.-8 p.m.
Still short of a few apple blue, sea green blocks? You can buy Lego blocks here by color. This store is also worth visiting for its amazing giant Lego sculptures. They change every season.

DISNEY STORE
1540 Broadway and W 46th St. on Times Square
stores.shopdisney.com
+1 212-626-2910
Mo.-Su. 8 a.m.-1 a.m.
Do you want a magical Disney experience? Go to the store just before it opens. You may just be the one chosen to unlock the doors with the magic key.

NEW YORK BABY

CHANGING DIAPERS: DOS AND DON'TS

There are a few shops where you can always go to change your baby's diapers.

An overview:
- Le Pain Quotidien. Very well equipped and very clean.
- McDonald's and Starbucks usually also have changing pads.
- Department stores such as Macy's, Bloomingdales or Saks Fifth Avenue all have a diaper-changing room.
- In an emergency, you could always try a hotel. They usually oblige.
- These days, more and more restaurants have a diaper-changing area. Almost everyone takes the baby along when they go out because the cost of both a dinner and sitter can get pretty high.
- Police stations can also be helpful. And that'll also give you a cool story to tell.

In the event of an 'accident', there's no shortage of shops where you can buy a new t-shirt. Babies don't always choose the most opportune moments to discharge their last meal. And yes, I speak from experience... But, hey, mishaps like this are always a good excuse for a new purchase. Fortunately Marie is now potty-trained. That fact alone is worth a dinner.

PORTABLE POTTY

Any ride on the subway can easily take more than an hour. That's a bit on the long side for a toddler who still doesn't have complete control of his bladder. So what do New York parents do? They just take a portable potty. One popular one is made by Oxo, for example. You can use it on top of a regular toilet or as a potty if you put a bag under it.

This is what many parents here do. So don't be surprised if you see an Upper East Side mom removing a portable potty from her Louis Vuitton Neverfull tote...

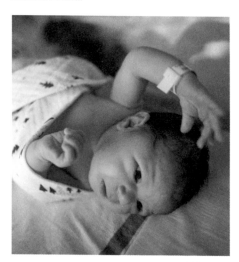

A TIP FROM PATRICK

Sometimes Marie gets startled when a toilet flushes automatically so I stick a Post-it on the sensor. That means the toilet flushes only after we've left and I've removed the Post-it.

A TIP FROM MARIE

Being born in New York may not be cheap but children often get discounts or even have free entry to museums and other cultural institutions. So before buying tickets, check first if children have to pay.

THE RIGHT TO BARE BREASTS

By law, breastfeeding is allowed everywhere in New York. Some women use a scarf or a shawl to cover themselves although they don't actually have to. In fact, you can even walk around topless in New York. That too is protected by law. Let me explain how that happened: women found it unfair that men were allowed to go topless on the street while women weren't, so in 1986 they started protesting in remarkable ways. Seven women held a topless picnic. At first they were arrested and charged but, in 1992, the court ruled in their favor and changed the law.

Since New York is so progressive when it comes to breastfeeding, every year during World Breastfeeding Week, a massive breastfeeding session is held in Times Square, where hundreds of women demonstrate how normal it is to nurse a baby in public.

NEW YO
IS WHE
THE FU
COMES
AUDITI

ORK

RE

TURE

TO

ON.

ED KOCH, MAYOR NY
(1978-1989)

LANGUAGES: ENGLISH AND CATALAN
FAVORITE PLAYGROUND: HIPPO PLAYGROUND AND CENTRAL PARK
HOBBY: BEING A MODEL AND MAKE-BELIEVE PHOTOGRAPHER
FAVORITE RESTAURANT: FRED'S
FAVORITE SHOP: BOOK CULTURE ON COLUMBUS
LIVES IN: UPPER WEST SIDE, MANHATTAN
FAVORITE WEBSITE: WWW.ROBERTCAPLIN.COM

MAX THE LITTLE COVER BOY

When I first came to live in New York I was so awestruck by the city that I immediately started taking pictures and shooting films. I like to watch professionals at work on YouTube and to learn from them. So you can imagine how happy I was when Robert Caplin agreed to do the photography for this book and promoted me to be his assistant. Needless to say, I didn't pass on this chance to learn from the best.

I got to know Robert when he took the photos for my first book, *BE NY From Tourist to New Yorker*. Now he has become a good friend. What has helped us bond is the fact that both of us have become fathers and never sleep. I mean: we've become fathers in the city that never sleeps. Or both. His son, Max, is probably one of the most photographed children in New York, despite his being only one year old.

Robert prefers taking pictures of his son, Max, in famous locations in the city. New York has a short history and it was only at the end of the 20th century that politicians and contractors realized that new is not always better. Renovation and restoration just happen to be more expensive than tearing down and building from scratch. Thanks to Jackie Kennedy, many splendid monuments such as Grand Central Terminal have been spared and are now being preserved for future generations.

'If we don't care about our past we can't have very much hope for our future'. With this strong message, Jackie gave New York a conscience. New buildings such as The Whitney Museum are, of course, very impressive, but it's mostly the established monuments that New Yorkers cherish most. The Chrysler Building, the New York Public Library on 42nd Street–these are the places where, for generations, people have come to take their family portraits. These are valuable memories and families always return to those locations for a picture when the next generation comes along. So take your time to immortalize your own family in front of one of the iconic buildings and start your own New York tradition. Your grandchildren and great-grandchildren will be very thankful because this will give them a reason to take their own children to New York.

⊜ A TIP FROM MAX

FRED'S
476 Amsterdam Ave., Upper West Side
www.fredsnyc.com
+1 212-579-3076
Su.-Th. 5 p.m-11 p.m., Fr.-Sa. 5 p.m.-12 a.m.
This restaurant has a canine theme.
The walls are covered in pictures of
cute doggies. No wonder it's Max's and
many other children's favorite place
on the Upper West Side.

⊜ A TIP FROM PATRICK

B&H
420 9th Ave. and W 34th St., Hudson Yards
www.bhphotovideo.com
+1 800-221-5743
Mo.-Th. 9 a.m.-7 p.m., Fr. 9 a.m.-2 p.m., Su. 10 a.m.-6 p.m.
Amateur photographer or cameraman? Then
you've got to reserve a few hours to wander
around B&H. The staff are all experienced
professionals so you will all speak the same language. This is the ultimate gadget store for adults
and it's my own guilty pleasure.

⊜ A TIP FROM ROBERT

ADORAMA
42 W 18th St., Flatiron District
www.adorama.com
+1 800-223-2500
Mo.-Th. 9 a.m.-8 p.m., Fr. 9 a.m.-5 p.m., Su.
9:30 a.m.-5 p.m.
From selfie sticks to professional gim-
bals, they have it all! If you ask Robert,
a visit to Adorama is a must for all
photographers, whether professional or amateur. Everything you need
(and much more) to take the perfect
picture.

TAKE ME A PICTURE

TIPS FOR TAKING PICTURES

New Yorkers are very friendly and will often offer to take a picture of you and your family. If that doesn't happen, just walk up to some cool-looking person: 'You look like you know how to take great pictures! Would you mind taking ours?' It would be a pity if someone were missing from the photo...

Look for a good backdrop. The skyline is always a hit, but the greenness of Central Park, the murals in SoHo or the graffiti in Bushwick all make for an impressive photo.

SAY CHEESE...

Like a real American, one of the first words Marie learned at the daycare center was *cheese*. And it had nothing to do with food.

ABC NYC

If you look around you'll see the streets are full of letters. Try taking photos of all the letters of the alphabet.

1, 2, 3 SCULPTURE

Look for the best sculptures and pose like the Statue of Liberty, the Charging Bull of Wall Street or the Angel of the Waters in Central Park.

—

SEND YOUR RESULTS TO PHOTO@BENY.BE OR #BENYFAMILY ON INSTAGRAM.

MOMMY/ DADDY AND ME CLASSES

Want to know what it's like to be a real New York mom or dad? Try taking a drop-in class. Here are a few we went to ourselves.

You can take a class for $25-$40 where you're also guaranteed to meet New York parents who can give you some free tips about their neighborhood.

MUSIC CLASS IN UPPER EAST SIDE

At TLB music you can take a music lesson in French ($35) or English ($25). Afterwards you could explore the neighborhood or visit one of the many museums on the Upper East Side.

ART CLASS IN GREENPOINT

Eckfort Art Studio
70 Eckfort St., Brooklyn

Artists aged 1 to 5 can come with their parents on Saturdays to create art between 9:30 and 11:30 a.m. ($27). You'll still have plenty of time to discover Greenpoint.

A TIP FROM INEKE

Almost every yoga studio in New York has several yoga classes a week for 'Mommy and Me.' Find a studio next to your hotel and go to a class with your baby or toddler. Marie has become a genuine yogi and likes to demonstrate how to do a downward facing dog.

DATE NIGHT

Anyone travelling with kids in New York probably wants at least one romantic evening as a couple. Just like ordering an Uber, in New York you can also order a babysitter using an app.

CHIME BY SITTERCITY

Chime by Sittercity is an app that lists only the best babysitters from the Sittercity website, after they have been screened. The super-sitters cost $17 an hour. There's an added $1 charge per extra child and the total is rounded up for the tip. Payment is by card.

LAST MINUTE: HELLO SITTER

It costs a bit more (starting at $21 an hour) but Hello Sitter allows you to book right up to the last minute. Kids already asleep and you want to go for a cocktail on a rooftop bar in the area? An hour later, the sitter is at your hotel door. You can book from a week before the date.

WHERE TO GO

Once the babysitter has been organized, these are the best places to go to:

ROOFTOPBAR
BOOM BOOM ROOM

The Standard, High Line,
848 Washington St.,
Meatpacking District
www.standardhotels.com
+1 212-645-4646
Su.-Tu. 4 p.m.-midnight,
We.-Sa. 4 p.m.-9 p.m.
Impressively attractive interior for a chic night out. The place to be for trendy New York. Even if you don't need to use the toilet, I recommend you go. Doubtless the most unique toilet experience of your life.

MU RAMEN

1209 Jackson Ave., LIC, Queens
www.ramennyc.wixsite.com/popup
+1 917-868-8903
Mo.-Su. 5 p.m-10 p.m.
Want to eat the best ramen (Japanese noodle soup) in New York? Do as the locals do and go to Mu Ramen in Queens. No tourists and the ramen is delicious. If you see me sitting there in my yellow shirt, don't hesitate to treat me to a sake to thank me for this priceless tip.

IPIC THEATER

11 Fulton St., South Street Seaport
www.ipictheaters.com
+1 212-776-8272
Mo.-Su. 10:30 a.m.-11:30 p.m.
A movie theater where you can sink into a leather sofa with a blanket and extra pillows while the waiter serves food prepared by a chef? It sounds too good to be true but it's exactly what you and your partner will find at iPic Theaters. Don't forget to make reservations.

VILLAGE VANGUARD

178 7th Ave. S, Greenwich Village
www.villagevanguard.com
+1 212-255-4037
Mo.-Su. 7:30 p.m.-2 a.m.
Nothing as romantic as going to a jazz club together in New York. If I want to treat Ineke, I take her to places like Village Vanguard. Great musicians like John Coltrane and Bill Evans performed here. Teenagers 13 and up are welcome.

LANGUAGES: <u>DANISH AND ENGLISH</u>
INSTAGRAM: @TRAVELINGWITHMARKUS
FAVORITE MUSEUM: <u>QUEENS MUSEUM</u>
FAVORITE PLAYGROUND: <u>IN REGO PARK (QUEENS)</u>
LIVES IN: <u>QUEENS</u>
WANTS TO BE: <u>LIMO DRIVER</u>

MARKUS KING OF QUEENS

My Danish co-guide, Maria Leena, lives with her son Markus (1.5) in Forest Hills in Queens. As a single parent, you sometimes have to be creative in New York. Fortunately, being a guide, Maria Leena is an expert on where to go in the city for fun but cheap excursions, such as often taking the ferry with Markus and knowing exactly which museums have a 'pay what you wish' entrance fee.

Mother and son like to go exploring in Corona Park, close to where they live. This park includes the New York Hall of Science, the Queens Zoo, the Queens Museum and the Unisphere. The latter was constructed for the 1964 New York World's Fair and is still the largest globe on this globe. It's a fitting symbol for Queens: this borough is one of the most diverse in the United States. About 50% of its inhabitants were born in another country. So for a delicious exotic meal, just hop on the subway and go to Queens. A trip to Latin America? In New York it's just a few subway stops away.

By living away from the center of the city, Maria Leena also saves on rent. The extra half-hour commute by subway is not a drawback for her. Before she's in the city she's been halfway around the world with a beaming Markus beside her.

As a tourist you can also take advantage of these perks. On the street you can have a Vietnamese eggroll as a starter, beef stroganoff as a main course, and Mexican churros for dessert, rounded off nicely with a Cuban cigar, all in a relaxed atmosphere and at an affordable price too. Instead of spending money on a cocktail in a fancy rooftop bar, she'd rather go with a girlfriend to an authentic bar in the neighborhood or enjoy a pizza in the park with Markus; the genuine New York experience.

That's the spirit: a hard day in New York is always a day in New York. That's worth a lot more to Maria Leena and Markus than a bursting bank account in Denmark.

☰ TIPS FROM MARKUS

FLUSHING MEADOWS - CORONA PARK

Queens New York
www.nycgovparks.org
Open 24 hours

Take the subway (7) to 111th Street in Queens straight to the park. You can easily spend the whole day here in the interesting museums and the Playground for All Children. This playground is suitable for both handicapped and able-bodied children.

QUEENS MUSEUM

Flushing Meadows, Corona Park, Queens
www.queensmuseum.org
+1 718-592-9700
We.-Su. 11 a.m.-5 p.m.

This museum houses the 'Panorama of the City of New York': a miniature replica of the whole city, constructed for the 1964 New York World's Fair. It's a unique opportunity for a good overview of the city and a whole lot cheaper than a helicopter ride. The entrance fee is by voluntary donation (suggested: $8, children free).

INEXPENSIVE NEW YORK

SUGGESTED ADMISSION

New York City has more than 700 galleries, 380 theater companies, 330 dance troupes, 131 museums, 96 orchestras, 40 Broadway theaters, 15 large concert halls, 5 zoos, 5 botanical gardens, and an aquarium. Many of these offer free admission at particular times or rely on voluntary donations.

A FEW FAVORITES:

NYC AQUARIUM

602 Surf Ave. and W 8th St., Coney Island, Brooklyn
www.nyaquarium.com
Sep. 5 to May 25: Mo.-Su. 10 a.m.-4:30 p.m. (last admission at 3:30 p.m.).
Summer: Mo.-Su. 10 a.m.-6 p.m. (last admission at 5 p.m.).
Want to stand face-to-face with sharks, sea otters, and clownfish? Then NYC Aquarium is the place to be. This is the oldest aquarium in the US. In the fall, winter and spring it's 'pay what you wish' on Fridays between 3 and 3:30 p.m. and in the summer between 4 and 5 p.m. Children under 3 can always enter for free.

FUN FACT
Afraid of sharks? In New York you are ten times more likely to be bitten by a person than by a shark.

BROOKLYN BOTANICAL GARDEN

990 Washington Ave., Prospect Park, Brooklyn
www.bbg.org
+1 718-623-7200
Dec. to Feb.: Tu.-Su. 10 a.m.-4:30 p.m.
March to Oct.: Tu.-Fr. 8 a.m.-6 p.m.,
Sa.-Su. 10 a.m.-6 p.m.
Relax in this beautiful botanical garden. Free for children under 12 years of age. In the winter there's free admission for all on weekdays and in the summer on Tuesdays and Saturdays between 10 a.m. and noon.

SOLOMON R. GUGGENHEIM MUSEUM

1071 5th Ave., between 88th St. and 89th St., Upper East Side
www.guggenheim.org
+1 212-423-3500
Su.-We. 10 a.m.-5:45 p.m., Fr. 10 a.m.-5:45 p.m., Sa. 10 a.m.-7:45 p.m.
This magnificent museum was designed by Frank Lloyd Wright and is definitely worth a visit. There's free admission on Saturdays between 5:45 and 7:45 p.m. Under-twelves get in free.

FUN FACT
Although the Guggenheim Museum houses works by famous artists such as Paul Gaugin and Pablo Picasso, it is mostly known for the building itself, which was designed by Frank Lloyd Wright. He drew 700 sketches before deciding on the famous spiral.

A DRINK ON THE FERRY

NYC FERRY
www.ferry.nyc
For only $2.75 you can call in at all kinds of additional places on the East River. From Astoria Queens to Roosevelt Island, Dumbo in Brooklyn, or even Rockaway Beach. Children under 44 inches can sail for free when accompanied by an adult. There's usually a small cafe/shop on board where you can get coffee, beer and wine. You can buy tickets at the vending machine or download the app (NYC Ferry).

FAMOUS BRIDGES: BMW
Three bridges connect Manhattan and Brooklyn: Brooklyn Bridge, Manhattan Bridge and Williamsburg Bridge. A good way to remember this, and in the right order, is by memorizing the name of the German car manufacturer BMW. The bridge connecting Manhattan and Queens is the Queensboro Bridge.

STORY TIME
When it gets cold in the winter–and in New York cold is really cold–shivering in the playground isn't much fun. That's why many parents go to story time in the libraries and bookstores, such as the New York Public Library, the Met, and most of the bookstores in Manhattan. Story time is more than just a reading. Songs are sung, finger puppets are made, and there is a variety of arts and crafts available. The latest craze is book readings by drag queens. Marie sometimes goes to one in the Court Square Library in Long Island City.

PIZZA ON THE WATERFRONT

SLICE
48-10 Vernon Blvd. and 48th Ave., Long Island City, Queens
www.slicelic.com
+1 718-937-5423
Su.-Th. 11 a.m.-2 a.m., Fr.-Sa. 11 a.m.-2 a.m.
Buy a slice of pizza at Slice and eat it on the waterfront in Hunter's Point South Park.

HUNTER'S POINT SOUTH PARK
Between the water and Center Blvd. from 46th Ave. to 54th Ave. in Long Island City, Queens
www.hunterspointparks.org
Mo.-Su. 6 a.m.-10 p.m.
This is one of the best spots for admiring the Manhattan skyline. There are playgrounds, lawns, and benches for your relaxation. We live nearby and the Rainbow Playground on the water at 47th Road is Marie's favorite. And ours too. It's a no brainer with a view like that.

A TIP FROM INEKE
MAHATTANHENGE
One of the most beautiful phenomena in New York is completely free. 'Manhattanhenge' is the urban version of Stonehenge. Twice a year (around May 29 and July 11) the sun sets exactly between the skyscrapers. On these evenings, New Yorkers all simply stand in the street, blocking the heavy Midtown traffic, whether it's to take pictures or just to enjoy this special moment. The best spots for observing this natural metropolitan event are on 14th, 23rd and 42nd Streets, as far east as possible, while still in sight of New Jersey. In LIC in Queens you can take great pictures without all the downtown bustle.

PICNIC PARKS

A TIP FROM PATRICK

PERFECT PICNIC NYC
81 Allen St., Little Italy
www.perfectpicnicnyc.com
+1 212-228-2884

A relaxing picnic in New York on a hot spring day? Perfect Picnic NYC takes care of it all. You can choose from a variety of picnic packages that are delivered to the park of your choice. Is that convenient or is that convenient?

FuN FACT

The only living cow in Manhattan is Othello. She lives in the Central Park Zoo. Thanks to Othello, New York kids can learn where milk comes from. And no, it's not from factories or delis.

CENTRAL PARK
59th St. to 110th St. between 5th and 8th Ave.
www.centralparknyc.org
Mo.-Su. 6 a.m.-1 a.m.

Without a doubt the most beautiful park in the world and there's always room to lie down somewhere. Need some children's activities? Have a look in the sheep meadow. Want to completely escape the city bustle? Then the Great Lawn at Turtle Pond is the ideal place, albeit for no other reason than spotting turtles...

☰ A TIP FROM PATRICK

CENTRAL PARK SIGHTSEEING
56 W 56th St., between 5th and 6th Aves., Midtown
And 5 other locations in Manhattan and Brooklyn
www.centralparksightseeing.com
+1 212-975-0785
Mo.-Su. 9 a.m.-5 p.m.

I hire all my bikes from Central Park
Sightseeing. They have bikes in all
sizes and even child seats. Marie got a
personalized seat for her first birthday
so she could always join the tours. She
already knows the route by heart. Just a
few more years and she can be the guide.
Central Park is surprisingly hilly. So
let the kids know there's
some heavy pedaling
coming. Worst case, you
can shorten the route.

WASHINGTON SQUARE PARK
Between 5th Ave. and Thompson St.,
Greenwich Village
www.nycgovparks.org
Open 24 hours

You'll always find a place to spread your
blanket and lie down in Washington
Square Park. But there's also a lot to do.
You'll probably hear musicians playing,
see artists making chalk drawings on
the ground, and more...
Every Wednesday from June to August
you can participate in children's yoga on
the grass between 10 and 10:45 a.m.

BRYANT PARK

Between W 40th St. and W 42nd St. and 5th and 6th Aves., Midtown

www.bryantpark.org

Mo.-Fr. 7 a.m.-midnight, Sa.-Su. 7 a.m.-11 p.m.

In the middle of all the Midtown madness it's great to unwind on the grass in Bryant Park. You can get something to eat at Whole Foods or at one of the many stalls in the park. And don't forget to take a couple of rides on the carousel. Marie just loves it.

FUN FACT

Throwing a coin into the fountain and making a wish brings good luck. You may like to know that, even if your wish doesn't come true, your money will be well spent. Every year about $4000 are collected in Bryant Park and used for its maintenance. So go ahead and make a couple of extra wishes.

FUN FACT

The best and cleanest public toilets can also be found in Bryant Park. You are welcomed by bouquets of real flowers and relaxing classical music. It's mostly because it's always so neat and clean that these toilets score so highly. Definitely worth a visit when nature calls or to prevent uncomfortable situations later during your walk.

FUN FACT

Under Bryant Park is the Public Library archive with more than 3 million books. It has seven underground stories.

EQUIPMENT LIST

A TIP
FROM PATRICK

FORTUNATELY IT ISN'T A DISASTER
IF YOU FORGET TO BRING
SOMETHING. JUST HAVE AMAZON
DELIVER IT TO YOUR HOTEL.

EXTRA CONVENIENT:

A FLASHLIGHT (FOR SEARCHING IN
YOUR SUITCASE AT NIGHT WHILE
EVERYBODY ELSE IS SLEEPING)

A UNIVERSAL TRAVEL ADAPTER PLUG

ONLY THE BEST FROM UPPER EAST TO UPPER WEST

(3-6 YEARS)

TODDLIN

2 AROUND

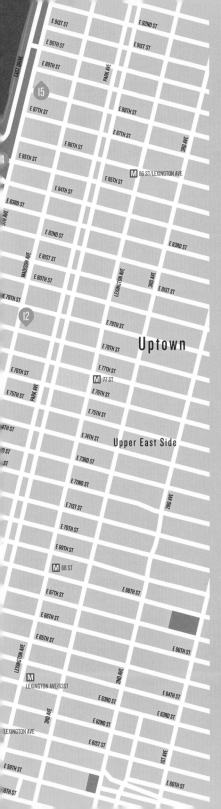

TODDLING AROUND

3-6 YEARS **+/- 5 MILES**

MIDTOWN – UPPER EAST SIDE –
CENTRAL PARK – UPPER WEST SIDE

<u>PART I: THE BEST FROM UPPER EAST</u>

1. THE PLAZA
2. APPLE FIFTH AVENUE
3. HORSE CARRIAGES
4. CENTRAL PARK ZOO
5. BALTO STATUE
6. BILLY JOHNSON PLAYGROUND
7. LIGHT POLES IN THE PARK
8. HANS CHRISTIAN ANDERSEN STATUE
9. MODEL BOAT SAILING
10. ALICE IN WONDERLAND
11. THE LOEB BOATHOUSE
12. LADY M CAKE BOUTIQUE
13. THE METROPOLITAN MUSEUM OF ART
14. ANCIENT PLAYGROUND
15. SOLOMON R. GUGGENHEIM MUSEUM

SEE NEXT PAGE → → →

TODDLING AROUND

3-6 YEARS **+/- 5 MILES**

MIDTOWN – UPPER EAST SIDE –
CENTRAL PARK – UPPER WEST SIDE

Toddling around is definitely the best way to explore the area around Central Park. New York is full of surprises. One moment you're drinking tea with Alice – the one from Wonderland – the next you're standing face to face with a grizzly.

This walk takes you on a journey through time. From the era of the dinosaurs, millions of years ago, to ancient Egypt, from The Beatles in the 20th century to the latest iPhone in our own 21st century. And you'll also encounter a time capsule that cannot be opened until the year 3000...

Live it up by climbing on statues, sailing in boats, trying out secret slides or taking a seat on a horse-drawn carriage when your tired legs can go no longer.

PART 1: THE BEST FROM UPPER EAST

📍 THE PLAZA

768 5th Ave.
www.fairmont.com
+1 212-759-3000
🕐 Open 24 hours

The Plaza Hotel has been world famous since the movie Home Alone 2. In the film, his parents absent, eight-year-old Kevin McCallister enjoys all the facilities the hotel has to offer, such as the ice cream sundae room service. Did you know there's an actual food market in the basement?

② APPLE FIFTH AVENUE

767 5th Ave.
www.apple.com
+1 212-336-1440
🕑 Open 24 hours

Jet lag or just can't sleep? The Apple Store is open day and night. Camping out at the front door for the latest iPhone is a yearly tradition here. You've got your sleeping bag, right?

③ HORSE CARRIAGES

E 59th St. and 5th Ave.
www.centralparksightseeing.com
+1 212-975-0785

Feel like a VIP as you are driven around Central Park in a horse-drawn carriage. Some coachmen present themselves as actual city guides but don't be fooled.

④ CENTRAL PARK ZOO

E 64th St. and 5th Ave.
www.centralparkzoo.com
+1 212-439-6500
🕑 Mo.-Su. 10 a.m.-4:30 p.m.,
$13-18, age two and under: free.

The nicest and certainly the softest New Yorkers can be found in this zoo. For instance, a grizzly bear or a snow leopard. Entry to the children's zoo is allowed only if you're accompanied by a child. The same goes for the playgrounds. Want to hear a hippo, a kangaroo, and a couple of monkeys play well-known children's songs? Then come to admire the magnificent Delacorte clock. You don't even have to enter the zoo to see it.

⑤ BALTO STATUE

Central Park, East Drive
www.centralparknyc.org
+1 212-310-6600
🕑 Mo.-Su. 6 a.m.-1a.m.

You can tell from this brave dog's shiny back and ears how many hugs he gets from all the children who come to visit him every day. Balto is a real hero. In 1925 he brought medicines for diphtheria and croup to Alaska, a more than 650-mile journey through heavy snowstorms.

FuNFACT

You can adopt a bench. You first buy a personalized plaque, which is then fixed to a bench. It costs $10,000 and the money goes towards the park's maintenance. To date, almost 50% of the 9000 benches have been adopted.

⑥ BILLY JOHNSON PLAYGROUND

Central Park, at E 67th St.
www.centralparknyc.org
+1 212-310-6600
🕑 Mo.-Su. 6 a.m.-1 a.m.

This is the first of the five playgrounds on this walk but easily one of the best, thanks to the most spectacular slide in Central Park.

⑦ LIGHT POLES IN THE PARK

Is your smartphone out of juice and you're afraid of getting lost? No problem. This trick will save you. All the 1600 light poles have a four-digit number. The first two refer to the nearest street. If the last two are an even number, then you're closer to East Side. Are they odd? Then you're closer to West Side.

FuNFACT

The park is 1.5 times bigger than Monaco.

⑧ HANS CHRISTIAN ANDERSEN STATUE

Central Park, at E 74th St.
www.centralparknyc.org
+1 212-310-6600
🕑 Mo.-Su. 6 a.m.-1 a.m.

Want a taste of what it was like to be a child? Go sit in the famous Danish author Hans Christian Andersen's lap and read the fairy tales in the book he's holding. I can assure you, you won't be the only one.

⑨ MODEL BOAT SAILING

Central Park, between E 72nd St. and
E 76th St.
www.sailthepark.com
+1 917-522-0054
🕐 Mo.-Th. 11 a.m.-5 p.m., Fr. 11 a.m.-7 p.m.,
Sa. 1 p.m-7 p.m., Su. 10 a.m.-6 p.m.,
$11 plus tax for a half hour.

Ship ahoy! All hands on
deck! In the summer, this is
a perfect place to relax for a
while. The kids can occupy
themselves for hours steer-
ing the model boats while
their parents sip their coffee at Le Pain Quotidien.

⑩ ALICE IN WONDERLAND

Central Park, at E 64th St.
www.centralparknyc.org
+1 212-310-6600
🕐 Mo.-Su. 6 a.m.-1 a.m.

Thanks to philanthropist
George Delacorte, children
can step into the world of
Lewis Caroll. This climb-
able statue of Alice and her
friends is one of Delacorte's
gifts to the children of
New York City. Nice detail:
the Mad Hatter is a carica-
ture of Delacorte himself.
The sculpture is also a tribute to his wife, Margarita,
who read Alice's Adventures
in Wonderland to their
children.

⑪ THE LOEB BOATHOUSE

Central Park, E 72nd St. and Park
Drive North
www.thecentralparkboathouse.com
+1 212-517-2233
🕐 Mo.-Su. 8 a.m.-5 p.m.,
$15 an hour.

Romantic rowing on the
lake? Not completely risk-
free: urban legend has it
that it's inhabited by giant
turtles. Many people dis-
posed of their unwanted
turtles here. With so much
space now, the turtles are
able to grow to enormous
proportions... Forewarned is
forearmed.

⑫ LADY M CAKE BOUTIQUE

41 E 78th St.
www.ladym.com
+1 212-452-222
🕐 Mo.-Fr. 10 a.m.-7 p.m., Sa. 11 a.m.-7 p.m.,
Su. 11 a.m.-6 p.m.

If you pile a thousand pancakes on top of each other
you get a delicious cake,
the famous *Mille Crêpes*.
New Yorkers will come
up with any excuse for a
celebration that calls for a
scrumptious piece of *Mille
Crêpes*.

⑬ THE METROPOLITAN MUSEUM OF ART

1000 5th Ave. and E 82nd St.,
Upper East Side
www.metmuseum.org
+1 212-731-1498
🕐 Su.-Th. 10 a.m.-5:30 p.m.,
Fr.-Sa. 10 a.m.-9 p.m.

This is the largest art museum in the United States.
It's so big that it can house a
complete Egyptian temple
and the permanent collec-
tion alone consists of more
than two million works
of art. So don't hesitate to
be selective about what
you want to see; otherwise
you'll be in there for days.

⑭ ANCIENT PLAYGROUND

Central Park, at E 84th St.
www.centralparknyc.org
+1 212-310-6600
🕐 Mo.-Su. 6 a.m.-1 a.m.

Squint a little and you're
time travelling through
Ancient Egypt. This
playground lets you climb
pyramids and plunge down
a slide, roam through the
tunnels, or build a sand
castle next to the obelisk.

⑥ SOLOMON R. GUGGENHEIM MUSEUM

1071 5th Ave.

www.guggenheim.org

+1 212-423-3500

🕐 Mo.-We. 10 a.m.-5:45 p.m.,
Fr. 10 a.m.- 5:45 p.m., Sa. 10 a.m.-
7:45 p.m., Su. 10 a.m.-5:45 p.m.

When President Trump
wanted to borrow a Van
Gogh, the curator said
it wasn't available at the
moment. She suggested
Trump take home *America*,
the 18 karat gold toilet by
artist Maurizio Cattelan,
which critics say is a
commentary on excessive
affluence in the US.
Besides its curator's sense
of humor, this museum is
mostly famous for its magnificent architecture by
Frank Lloyd Wright.

PART 2: THE BEST FROM UPPER WEST

① DELACORTE THEATER

81 Central Park West

www.publictheater.org

+1 212-539-8500

In the summer, this well-
known open-air theater
features Shakespeare in
the Park. Tickets are free
but to get them you need
to stand in line for a long
time the day before the
performance.

② SWEDISH COTTAGE MARIONETTE THEATRE

W 79th St. in Central Park

www.cityparksfoundation.org

In the middle of Central
Park you'll find this
charming, fairytale-like
puppet theater where the
puppets will literally break
into song and dance. The
marionette company has
long been known for its
playful productions of
children's classics such as
Peter Pan and Cinderella.

③ BELVEDERE CASTLE

Central Park, at 79th St.

www.centralparknyc.org

+1 212-310-6600

🕐 Mo.-Su. 6 a.m.-1 a.m.

This picturesque folly has
been home to the Central
Park weather station since
1919, but among Smurf
fans it's better known as
Gargamel's castle. But don't
expect to find him at home.
They do have a visitors' center and a souvenir shop.

FUNFACT

Central Park has appeared
in more than 350 movies. It
has also been dubbed 'world's
most-filmed city park.'

④ AMERICAN MUSEUM OF NATURAL HISTORY

Central Park West, between W 71st St.
and W 81st St.

www.amnh.org

🕐 Mo.-Su. 10 a.m.-5:45 p.m.

This is where little New
Yorkers learn everything
about the world around
them. It's popular chiefly
for its many dinosaurs.
Everything you've always
wanted to know about
planets, mummies, or the
oceans can be found here.

⑤ BOOK CULTURE ON COLUMBUS

450 Columbus Ave.

www.bookculture.com

+1 212-595-1962

🕐 Mo.-Sa. 9 a.m.-10 p.m.,
Su. 9 a.m.-8 p.m.

You'd never know by
looking at it from the outside, but this bookstore's
basement is a children's
paradise for playing and
reading. Reading hour is
not just in English, but also
in other languages, such as
Spanish, Russian, Hindi,
and French.

6 SHAKE SHACK

366 Columbus Ave.
www.shakeshack.com
+1 646-747-8770
🕐 Mo.-Su. 10:30 a.m.-11 p.m.
Possibly the most re-
nowned hamburgers in
New York, though the
ribbed fries and the yum-
my shakes are at least as
popular.

7 COUTURE KIDS

324 Columbus Ave.
www.couturekids.nyc
+1 212-362-3200
🕐 Mo.-Sa. 10 a.m.-7 p.m., Su. 11 a.m.-6 p.m.
Looking for a Fendi
Dress or child-size
Roberto Cavalli suit? Or
is it your dream to parade
around the beach with your
daughter or son in match-
ing Vilebrequin swimsuits?
Hopefully you've set aside
a hefty sum for souvenirs;
otherwise your budget will
be used up right away.

8 SWEETGREEN

311 Amsterdam Ave.
www.sweetgreen.com
+1 212-496-4081
🕐 Mo.-Su. 10:30 a.m.-10 p.m.
New York is a mecca not
only for junk food, but
also for healthy meals.
Sweetgreen is one of our
favorites, especially be-
cause you can choose your
own salad ingredients.

9 LEVAIN BAKERY

167 W 74th St.
www.levainbakery.com
+1 212-874-6080
🕐 Mo.-Sa. 8 a.m.-7 p.m., Su. 9 a.m.-7 p.m.
This joint came into being
after two friends decided
to make the world's best
chocolate chip cookie.
According to The New York
Times they succeeded in
their mission. There are
many varieties and they're
all equally delicious. The
chocolate chip walnut is
particularly popular among
New Yorkers.

10 ALICE TEA CUP

102 W 73rd St.
www.aliceteacup.com
+1 212-799-3006
🕐 Mo.-Su. 8 a.m.-8 p.m.
Now that you've already
climbed the mushrooms
in Wonderland with Alice,
it's time for tea and scones,
sandwiches, or pancakes...
Don't forget to put on
your wings because only
real fairies come here to
drink tea.

11 THE DAKOTA

1 W 72nd St.
This is where John Lennon,
the Beatles' singer-song-
writer, lived and where he
was shot and killed at his
front door. Every day, doz-
ens of fans gather here, at
the scene of the tragedy.

12 STRAWBERRY FIELDS

Central Park, at W 72nd St.
www.centralparknyc.org
+1 212-310-6600
🕐 Mo.-Su. 6 a.m.-1 a.m.
This is the John Lennon
memorial in Central Park
with, at its center, the
wonderful Imagine mosaic.
There are always musicians
playing Beatles numbers
here. Thanks to the film
The Boss Baby, even Marie
can sing along to *Blackbird*.

13 TOTS PLAYGROUND

Central Park, at W 67th St.
www.centralparknyc.org
+1 212-310-6600
🕐 Mo.-Su. 6 a.m.-1 a.m.
You can swing, build sand
castles, and learn to climb
in this playground. The
choice location for Upper
West Side tots and toddlers
for a playdate with their
friends.

⑭ ADVENTURE PLAYGROUND

Central Park, at W 67th St.
www.centralparknyc.org
+1 212-310-6600
🕐 Mo.-Su. 6 a.m.-1 a.m.

For older kids, who are more adventurous. Besides a fort, there's also a maze and there's so much to climb that it could be a great training camp for a Mount Everest expedition.

⑮ TAVERN ON THE GREEN

Central Park West and 67th St.
www.tavernonthegreen.com
+1 212-877-8684
🕐 Mo.-Th. 11 a.m.-4 p.m. and 5 p.m.-9 p.m., Fr. 11 a.m.-4 p.m. and 5 p.m.-11 p.m., Sa. 9 a.m.-4 p.m. and 5 p.m.-11 p.m., Su. 9 a.m.-4 p.m. and 5 p.m.-9 p.m.

Tavern on the Green was originally designed as a safe haven for the 700 sheep that grazed in Sheep Meadow. The sheep have been moved to more pleasant pastures and Sheep Meadow is now a peaceful picnic field. Tavern on the Green has been converted into a restaurant. If you dine here, you may just happen to sit on a seat once occupied by a character from one of the more than twenty movies that have been shot here, such as *New York, I Love You, Alfie* and *The Out-of-Towners*.

⑯ CENTRAL PARK CAROUSEL

1802 65th St. Transverse
www.centralparknyc.org
+1 212-439-6900
🕐 Mo.-Su. 10 a.m.-6 p.m.
$3 a ride.

After a ride in a horse-drawn carriage, get on a horse of your own here. Choose one of the 57 colorful steeds... and they're off!

⑰ HECKSCHER PLAYGROUND

Central Park, at W 62nd St. and 7th Ave.
www.centralparknyc.org
+1 212-310-6600
🕐 Mo.-Su. 6 a.m.-1 a.m.

I saved the biggest and oldest playground for last. A favorite especially in the summer due to its imaginative water games, though it can get very busy. Follow the water through the canals or soak everyone by squirting them with the water jets.

⑱ COLUMBUS CIRCLE

848 Columbus Circle
🕐 Open 24 hours

The famous globe is the geographical center of New York. So if you read that Brussels is 3657 miles from New York or Los Angeles 2797 miles, then you know that's the distance to the center of Columbus Circle.

Columbus Circle is also the location of one of the many Trump Towers and of CNN headquarters. The Time Warner Center's stores are a great place to go shopping. The first Amazon store is also located here. Below ground you'll find the Turnstyle, a market with shops and food stalls. You can eat or shop here without even taking your subway card out of your pocket.

LIKES: <u>A RIDE ON THE MERRY-GO-ROUND</u>

LANGUAGES: <u>ENGLISH, DUTCH, SPANISH</u>

WANTS TO BE: <u>SKYSCRAPER BUILDER OR PASTRY CHEF</u>

FAVORITE FOOD: <u>BUNNY-SHAPED PIZZAS AT ROSSOPOMODORO</u>

FAVORITE SECRET PLACE: <u>THE SPRINKLERS ON THE ROOF OF THE AMERICAN MUSEUM OF NATURAL HISTORY</u>

FAVORITE BOOKSTORE: <u>STORY TIME AT THE NEW YORK PUBLIC LIBRARY</u>

INSTAGRAM: <u>@MARIEANDWE</u>

LIVES IN: <u>LONG ISLAND CITY, QUEENS</u>

MARIE A BUBBLE OF HAPPINESS

I had been living in New York for seven years when my daughter Marie was born. Being a guide was becoming second nature to me so I never expected this lambkin could make me an even better guide. But she did. Children see the city in a different way. Not only from their physically lower vantage point but also by what attracts their attention and whose attention they themselves attract. In New York everybody is always in transit. For Marie (now 3) a subway ride is one of the day's highlights. She says hello to everyone and, to my great surprise, everyone says something back. New Yorkers unfriendly? Forgettaboutit!

People sometimes ask about the best time of year to visit New York, but that's difficult to answer. There's something to be said for every season. Don't stay cooped up in your hotel room, even if it's 90° in the summer or if it's raining cats and dogs in the fall, or if the streets are blanketed in white in the winter and New York resembles a fairytale land. Our apartment (luxury shoebox, that is) isn't much bigger than a hotel room and with a small child there's no choice but to go outside. When we took the subway to Manhattan with Marie on a drizzly day, everyone was just staring into space. Until Marie started laughing. Before you knew it, a spontaneous conversation had begun among the passengers. At the next stop someone said that a 'bubble of happiness' had materialized around Marie, and he was right. I'd noticed it before. New Yorkers are very sympathetic to children and are always considerate to young parents. They gladly give up their seat on the subway, even to a man with a carrier bag, or they help carry the stroller to the platform despite all the steps they have to brave. How amazing is that?

On rainy days we like to go to Oculus, the new World Trade Center station by the Spanish architect Santiago Calatrava. Marie can carelessly run around without getting wet, the architecture is magnificent and while we're there we can shop around in the mall or have a delectable cake at Lady M. You see, the best medicine for bad weather blues in New York is 'retail therapy': 3, 2, 1... on your marks, credit cards set, go... shopping. If you'd rather spend less money, Grand Central Terminal is a good option, where you can see the miniature trains in the MTA Museum or the real ones on the platform.

Snow in New York has something magical about it. A white muffling blanket is spread over the city. Suddenly all's still. You can make snow angels in the middle of the busy streets until the snowplows clear the way. After a walk in Central Park, it's great to get warm again in the Metropolitan Museum of Art, one of the largest, most important art museums in the world. Happiness is soaking up some art while your fingers and toes defrost.

New York may get extremely cold in the winter but it can also get extremely hot in the summer, when all those ➜ ➜

stone buildings absorb the heat. But don't worry: even during heat waves you can swim for free in one of the many public open-air pools. Marie's favorite place to get cool is the roof of The American Museum of Natural History because she can combine a refreshing shower in the sprinklers with a visit to the museum's dinosaurs.

⊜ TIPS FROM MARIE

NEW YORK PUBLIC LIBRARY
476 5th Ave., at E 41st St., Midtown
www.nypl.org
Mo.-Sa. 10 a.m.-5:45 p.m., Su. 1 p.m.-5 p.m.
If you want to meet the one and only Winnie the Pooh, go to the Children's Center's play and reading corner. You can get there via the entrance on 42nd Street (first right) in Room 84 on the ground floor. The rest of the library is also worth visiting, especially the well-known Rose Main Reading Room.

ROSSOPOMODORO
118 Greenwich Ave. and W 13th St., Greenwich Village
www.rossonyc.com
Mo.-Fr. noon-4 p.m. and 5 p.m.-11 p.m., Sa.-Su. 11 a.m.-4 p.m. and 5 p.m.-11 p.m.
Delicious Italian Cuisine. On weekends, children can choose their pizza's shape. Marie always goes for a bunny. Reservations are recommended if you want to make sure you get a table. Don't confuse this restaurant with the Pomodoro Rosso, which became known as the 'break-up restaurant' in *Seinfeld*.

FUN FACT
When The Stephen A. Schwarzman Building (the main building of The New York Public Library) was built in 1911, it was the largest marble building in the United States.

FUN FACT
The New York Public Library is a popular set for movies and TV series. From *Breakfast at Tiffany's* to *Spider-Man*, from *Ghostbusters* to *The Thomas Crowne Affair* and *Sex and the City*.

NEW YORK CITY OR MUSEUM CITY?

Walk up any street and you'll find a museum. Next to the famous ones, such as The Metropolitan Museum, The Whitney Museum and the MoMA, there's also, for instance, the Houdini Museum, the Museum of the American Gangster, and the Skyscraper Museum. You could, of course, say that New York City already is a skyscraper museum, but this one is for those who really can't get enough of them...

THE MUSEUM OF MODERN ART (MOMA)
11 W 53rd St., between 5th and 6th Aves., Midtown
www.moma.org
+1 212-708-9400
Sa.-Th. 10:30 a.m.-5:30 p.m., Fr. 10:30 a.m.-8 p.m.

Of all the museums in New York we like to go to the MoMA the most. We even have a membership. Though I must admit the membership is also appealing for the discounts it offers at the magnificent gift shop. The temporary exhibitions are never disappointing but we can never enter the MoMA without taking a look at Monet's *Water Lilies* or Van Gogh's *The Starry Night*.
Marie likes the Art Lab the most (go through the garden and then back inside on the right) because she can create her own art there. Admission is free on Fridays between 4 and 8 p.m. and always for children under 16.

FUN FACT
Since 1985, the artist Adrian Piper has been collecting her clipped nails and hair cuttings in jars. When a jar is full it's added to her artwork in the MoMA.

CHILDREN'S MUSEUM OF MANHATTAN
212 W 83rd St., between Broadway and Amsterdam Ave., Upper West Side
www.cmom.org
+1 212-721-1223
Tu.-Fr. 10 a.m.-5 p.m., Sa. 10 a.m.-7 p.m., Su. 10 a.m.-5 p.m.

This museum has five stories and they're all great. Pretend you're driving a fire truck or that you are The President of the United States of America. Admission is free on the first Friday of every month between 5 and 8 p.m. This museum is mostly suitable for ages anywhere between 0 and 12.

AMERICAN MUSEUM OF NATURAL HISTORY
Central Park West, between W 79th St. and W 81st St., Upper West Side
www.amnh.org

This museum is mostly renowned for its dinosaurs, the life-sized giant blue whale, and the Hayden planetarium. Are you here in the summer? Don't miss out on cooling off in the sprinklers on the roof.
Tip: If it's very busy use the side entrance or the entrance at the back of the building.

FUN TRIVIA ABOUT THE AMERICAN MUSEUM OF NATURAL HISTORY

Every year in September the model of the giant blue whale – the largest animal alive today – is cleaned with giant vacuum cleaners. You can watch this on the museum's YouTube channel.

President Theodore Roosevelt made a donation to the museum of an elephant he himself had shot. This colossal creature can be seen at the Akeley Hall of African Mammals.

In 1964 two professional thieves broke into the museum. They escaped with 3 million dollars' worth of jewels. A few gems were later recovered but the Eagle diamond is still missing.

The museum's collection includes the world's largest meteorite. It landed on earth about 10,000 years ago.

Located next to the entrance on Columbus Avenue is The New York Times Capsule, designed by the Spanish architect Santiago Calatrava, who also created the new World Trade Center station, Oculus. The capsule was sealed in 2000 and will only be opened in the year 3000. Excited about developments in medicine? Pass it on in your genes because only your great-great-great-great (etc.) grandchildren will be able to witness the event.

You can stay overnight in the museum, just like in the movie *Night at the Museum*. This is possible only a couple of nights each year and costs $145 per person. Reservations are a must.

ON THE MERRY-GO-ROUND

CENTRAL PARK CAROUSEL
Middle of Central Park, at 64th St.
Mo.-Su. 10 a.m.-6 p.m.
With 57 horses, this merry-go-round is one of the largest in America. It's said that, in 1870, the Park's very first carousel was pulled by a horse.

SEAGLASS CAROUSEL, BATTERY PARK
State St. & Water St., Financial District
Su.-Th. 10 a.m.-7 p.m., Fr.-Sa. 10 a.m.-8 p.m.
This merry-go-round is truly magical. It's like you're underwater among the most amazing fish. Even adults are willing to stand in line to enter this underwater fairytale.

LE CARROUSEL, BRYANT PARK
85 W 40th St., Midtown
www.bryantpark.org
Mo.-Fr. 10 a.m.-midnight, Sa.-Su. 10 a.m.-11 p.m.
I just love it when Ineke and Marie wait for me in Bryant Park after a hard day's work at my BelCham office on 6th Avenue. A visit to the merry-go-round has become customary. Among the horsies there's also one rabbit. Three guesses which animal Marie always wants to ride. Yep. Sometimes we have to wait for a while before the bunny is free.

JANE'S CAROUSEL, BROOKLYN BRIDGE PARK
Old Dock St., at the waterside, Dumbo, Brooklyn
Th.-Su. 11 a.m.-6 p.m.
This merry-go-round gives you a free bonus view of the Manhattan skyline and Brooklyn Bridge. With a bit of luck you'll see newly-weds taking their wedding pictures, just like Ineke and I did right here. We always celebrate our wedding anniversary by riding the carousel with Marie and being whirled back in time for a short moment.

IN NY,
FAMILY
ARE ENC
ANYWHE
ANYTIM

HUGS

OURAGED,

RE,

LANGUAGES: ENGLISH, FRENCH AND KOREAN
FAVORITE PLACE: SWEDISH COTTAGE MARIONETTE THEATRE IN CENTRAL PARK
FAVORITE PLAYGROUND: THE HIGHLINE
HOBBIES: FRENCH, TAEKWONDO, DRAWING, PAINTING AND PLAYING THE CELLO
CREATIVE HANGOUT: CHILDREN'S MUSEUM OF THE ARTS
FAVORITE SNACK: SEAWEED AND AGED DUTCH CHEESE
FAVORITE RESTAURANT: PIACERE
LIVES IN: WEST VILLAGE

BLUE
MY SOMETHING BLUE

Swooning over a romantic movie situated in New York, you'd think finding Mr. or Mrs. Right in New York is a piece of cake. You just never know when it will happen. I got to know my wife, Ineke, on one of my tours. Just like in the movie Serendipity, we fell in love while walking together through Central Park. It can't get more romantic than that. As with all happy endings, there was also a wedding. According to tradition, the bride must bring something old, something new, something borrowed, and something blue. The last one was easy. My best friend Christian's cute son's name is Blue so we asked him to carry the ring. So Ineke had her something blue and nine months later, when our daughter Marie was born, she immediately had Blue as her very first friend.

Like many children in New York, Blue (5) is the product of two very talented parents. Christian has his own design studio,

Kitchen NY, and has already won the Cannes Lions award, the design world's Oscar, twice. Lucia is a pianist. She and both her sisters, who play violin and cello, studied at The Juilliard School, which only admits the world's best musicians. As the Ahn Trio they now perform all over the world. They even played for President Obama.

So it's no surprise that Blue is also a great little guy. Every morning he walks to school on the High Line while talking to his dad about everything that occupies him. But his favorite day is Saturday because that's when he hits the city with Christian and Lucia. A promenade on the Brooklyn Bridge, a visit to the Children's Museum of the Arts or a show at the puppet theater in Central Park. Blue absorbs it all like a true New Yorker. And since his parents like to discover new restaurants and cool neighborhoods, Blue may one day become a really good guide...

⊜ TIPS FROM BLUE

SWEDISH COTTAGE MARIONETTE THEATRE
W 79th St. in Central Park
www.cityparksfoundation.org
A puppet theater right in the middle
of Central Park. A unique theater in
a unique location. The show alter-
nates several times a year. Want to see
rapping hip-hop puppets? Check the
website and reserve your tickets well
in advance.

FꞟN FACT
The Swedish Cottage Marionette Theatre
was originally a gift from Sweden in 1876.
For some time, it was used as a public
toilet, prompting Sweden to threaten to
take it back. It was quickly reinstated.

CHILDREN'S MUSEUM OF THE ARTS
103 Charlton St., between Greenwich St.
and Hudson St., Tribeca
www.cmany.org
+1 212-274-0986
Mo. noon-5 p.m., Tu.-We. closed, Th.-Fr.
noon-6 p.m., Sa.-Su. 10 a.m.-5 p.m.
This is where creative children can
really indulge themselves.
On Thursdays between 4 and 6 p.m.
you can decide your own entrance
fee. Making monsters out of clay,
being covered in slime or painting like
Picasso – you can do it all here.

LINCOLN CENTER
10 Lincoln Center Plaza, Upper West Side
www.lincolncenter.org/kids
Lincoln Center has a variety of performances
for children. From classical music for babies to
stories and plays for tots. Even the New York
Philharmonic plays for schoolchildren.
These concerts are very popular among little
New Yorkers so make sure you order your
tickets in time.

⊜ A TIP FROM PATRICK

PIACERE
351 Broome St., between Elisabeth St. and Bowery, Little Italy
www.piacerenyc.com
+1 212-219-4080
Mo.-Su. noon-1 a.m.
Anyone dreaming of becoming
a top chef? At Piacere, children can
make and eat their own pizza. Blue and Marie
have lived it up here plenty of times.

WILL YOU MARRY ME?

Hurray! You've found the love of your life! If you propose in New York you immediately have the ideal excuse to come back every year.

THE BEST PLACES TO PROPOSE

Typically New York, but no less romantic therefore, is being proposed to while rowing a boat in Central Park or while skating at Rockefeller Center. But, in my opinion, the best place will always be the rooftop bar of The Standard. That's where I asked Ineke to marry me, with a view of the whole city.

GETTING MARRIED IN NY

First, you have to request a Marriage License. This can be done for $35 at the Marriage Bureau on 141 Worth St. from 60 days before the wedding date. There's a mandatory 'second-thoughts period' of at least 24 hours between the application and the wedding day.

IN THE OFFICE OF THE CITY CLERK
141 Worth St., between Center St. and Baxter St., Financial District
www.cityclerck.nyc.gov
+1 212-669-8090
Mo.-Fr. 8:30 a.m.-3:45 p.m.

Contrary to popular belief, you don't get married in City Hall itself. You can go for a ceremony at the Office of the City Clerk. That's what Ineke and I did. You bring your ID, a witness, and 25 dollars. What's nice is that you don't have to make an appointment. You draw a number, as if you were at the butcher's, and watch all the other couples getting married until it's your turn. What an experience. Worth going even if you aren't getting married. Don't be shocked if after all that, the ceremony takes only 90 seconds.

THE NAKED COWBOY IN TIMES SQUARE
Times Square, Midtown
www.nakedcowboy.com/weddings

You could always decide to get married somewhere else but then you have to hire a marriage celebrant. They will make sure all the paperwork is in order and is taken to the City Clerk's office. The official papers will be sent to you within 30 days. Try the Naked Cowboy. He'll only charge you $499.

AT THE EMPIRE STATE BUILDING WITH ST. VALENTINE
350 5th Ave., between W 33rd St. and W 34th St., Midtown
www.esbnyc.com
Mo.-Su. 8 a.m.-2 a.m.

Each year an exceptional contest is held. The winning fourteen couples get to wed on top of the Empire State Building on the most romantic day of the year: St. Valentine's Day.

FUN FACT

The Belgian-American fashion designer Diane von Fürstenberg married Barry Diller at the City Clerk's Office on February 2, 2001. John Legend and Chrissy Teigen also got married there. So if you're lucky, you might spot a celebrity.

A TIP FROM INEKE

Whatever you buy, never say it's for your wedding. If you mention the word 'wedding' prices double on the spot.

'SAY YES TO THE DRESS'
KLEINFELD BRIDAL
110 W 20th St., Flatiron District
www.kleinfeldbridal.com
By appointment.
If you want to get married in New York and also buy your dress there, you should make the appointment before you book your trip: this bridal store is world famous thanks to the TV reality show *Say Yes to the Dress*.

ROMANTIC FILM SETS IN NEW YORK

BREAKFAST AT TIFFANY'S
TIFFANY & CO: THE BLUE BOX CAFÉ
727 5th Ave. and E 57th St., Midtown
www.tiffany.com
+1 212-755-8000
Mo.-Sa. 10 a.m.-7 p.m., Su. noon-6 p.m.
This year for Halloween Marie dressed up as Holly Golightly (Audrey Hepburn in *Breakfast at Tiffany's*). Partly due to the new cafe at Tiffany's on 5th Avenue, this classic movie is totally in again. Go there for breakfast in style.

SERENDIPITY
SERENDIPITY 3
225 E 60th St., between 2nd and 3rd Aves., Upper East Side
www.serendipity3.com
+1 212-838-3531
Sa.-Th. 10:30 a.m.-midnight, Fr. 10:30 a.m.-1 a.m.
There are still long lines to the restaurant featured in this movie. On holidays, a wait of four hours is not uncommon. Treat yourself to a milkshake when you're finally inside – they're certainly worth the wait.

FUN FACT
Every year a competition is held in which fashion designers make a wedding gown from toilet paper instead of from shiny fabric. More than 1500 designers participate. The first prize is $10,000 and the winning dress is displayed in Ripley's Believe It or Not! Times Square.

FUN FACT
Serendipity 3 got into Guinness World Records for their *Frrrozen 'Haute' Chocolate Dessert*. However, the dessert costs $25,000. But it does come with a diamond bracelet and a gold spoon. Thinking about it? Let them know in time because the cocoa has to be flown in from several continents.

NY STYLE PIZZA

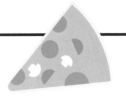

SEE MORE ON
BENY
Minute
▶/BENYMINUTE

HOW DO YOU EAT A NY SLICE?

New York pizza is so good; you've got to go for it first thing. Just make sure you don't burn your mouth. You can do this by folding the pizza in two. This also keeps you from getting messy because it prevents the grease from leaking. It's a quickly learned skill; even Marie already consumes her pizza like a real New Yorker. She's certainly had lots of practice.

THE FIRST: LOMBARDI'S

32 Spring St. and Mott St., SoHo
www.firstpizza.com
+1 212-941-7994
Su.-Th. 11:30 a.m.-11 p.m., Fr.-Sa. 11:30 a.m.-midnight
Probably the United States' first pizzeria. Gennaro Lombardi was an immigrant from Naples who sold whole pizzas for 5 cents in 1905. But since that was too expensive for many people, it wasn't long before slices were sold too. The pizza here is still delicious, as is the ambience.

THE CHEAPEST: 2 BROS PIZZA

31 W 46th St., between 5th and 6th Aves., Midtown
And eight other locations in Manhattan
www.2brospizza.com
+1 212-704- 4251
Mo.-Su. 10 a.m.-2 a.m.
You can get a good slice of pizza at 2 Bros for as little as $1. Their secret? They simply sell tons of pizzas and your slice is never limp from waiting for hours to be bought.

THE BEST: ROBERTA'S

261 Moore St. and Bogard St., Bushwick, Brooklyn
Mo.-Fr. 11 a.m.-midnight, Sa.-Su. 10 a.m.-midnight
230 Park Avenue in Urban Space Vanderbilt
Mo.-Fr. 6:30 a.m.-9 p.m., Sa.-Su. 9 a.m.-5 p.m.
www.robertaspizza.com
Many New Yorkers will tell you Roberta's is the best pizza in town. I totally agree. So I was really happy when they came to the Food Hall, Urban Space Vanderbilt in Manhattan. Though a trip to Bushwick is always fun.

THE MOST ORIGINAL: TWO BOOTS

558 Driggs Ave., Williamsburg, Brooklyn
And seven other locations in Manhattan and Brooklyn
www.twoboots.com
+1 718-387-2668
Mo.-Th. 11 a.m.-11 p.m., Fr. 11 a.m.-3 a.m.,
Sa. 11:30 a.m.-3 a.m., Su. noon-10:30 p.m.
Two Boots pizza is a successful combination of Cajun (Southern Louisiana) and Italian. There are several branches around the city and every Two Boots has its own specialty. But more importantly you can buy it by the slice, which is the New York way.

FUN FACT

Experts say the reason the pizza in New York is so good is the fresh water streaming in from the Catskill Mountains, 125 miles away.

FUN FACT

The drinking water in New York contains tiny shrimps, which aren't harmful to your health.

FAVORITE BROADWAY MUSICAL: THE LION KING AND FROZEN
FAVORITE SHOP: BROOKLYN OWL
FAVORITE SNACK: CUPCAKES FROM BAKED BY MELISSA AND TAIYAKI MILKSHAKES
FAVORITE RESTAURANT: SHAKE SHACK
HOBBIES: BALLET, DANCING, SINGING, SWIMMING, DRAWING, AND CRAFTS
LIVE IN: MAPLEWOOD, NEW JERSEY

LILY AND EVIE FAMOUS TWINS

On Sundays I like to take my clients to gospel churches. These churches, full of singing and praying people who are in no hurry to get the service over with, are a nice contrast to the hectic life on the street. Time is money, New Yorkers say, so they usually have no time to waste, except when they're in church, because a moment of reflection takes way more than just five minutes. I only go into gospel churches as part of my work as a city guide but that's not the case with my friend and colleague Daniel. For him, a visit to the church is a truly religious experience.

And he communicates that to his children. I really admire him, because besides being a guide he's also a true family man. He and his wife have one son, Josiah, twins Lily and Evie (4) as well as two dachshunds, Max and Bella. A typical American family, in other words. Also because a couple of years ago they moved to Maplewood, a picturesque village in New Jersey.

I already wrote about Daniel in my first book: he's a born entertainer who is not only a history major but has also graduated as an actor. It was his dream to make it in the movies or on stage in New York, but eventually he realized that being a guide was what really made him happy. New York is a mecca for film buffs. When you first come to New York, many streets and buildings will look familiar, which should come as no surprise when you consider that every year more than 250 movies and TV shows are shot there.

One of those movies is *Tallulah*, a romantic comedy from 2016 directed by Sian Heder, in which a Manhattan mother hires someone to babysit her toddler. The child's part is played by Daniel's twins. Lily and Evie took turns playing the role of the whining brat. No-one noticed that the part was actually played by two girls and Daniel was bursting with pride about his daughters' acting skills. New York also plays a leading role in the movie–the city is shown in all its glory.

If you want to discover New York as a (wannabe?) movie star, you must go for a walk, a jog, or a picnic in Central Park, one of the most-filmed areas in Manhattan. Movies like *Home Alone 2, The Smurfs* and *Spider-Man* all take place there. What's nice is that you sometimes literally bump into an actor there. For example, Tom Hanks jogs there once in a while. One time he accidentally appeared in the wedding photo of a couple who had chosen Central Park as the setting for their wedding pictures. Proof that even celebrities like to photo-bomb.

☰ A TIP FROM DANIEL

BROOKLYN TABERNACLE
17 Smith St., Brooklyn Heights, Brooklyn
www.brooklyntabernacle.org
+1 718-290-2000
The best place to experience a gospel
service. Don't be shy, gear up those
vocal chords and let it rip.

FüNFACT

In New York it's a misdemeanor to
deliberately break wind in a church. If you're
out of luck there'll be a cop sitting next to
you and you'll get fined.

☰ A TIP FROM LILY

BAKED BY MELISSA
1585 Broadway, Times Square
And nine other locations in Manhattan
www.bakedbymelissa.com
Mo.-Fr. 8 a.m.-midnight, Sa. 10 a.m.-midnight,
Su. 10 a.m.-11 p.m.
The mini-cupcakes are tiny and cute,
perfect for a celebration.

☰ A TIP FROM EVIE

SHAKE SHACK
Madison Ave. and E 23rd St. in Madison Square Park,
Flatiron District
And 11 other locations in Manhattan
www.shakeshack.com
Mo.-Fr. 7:30 a.m.-11 p.m., Sa.-Su. 8:30 a.m.-11 p.m.
Evie particularly likes the homemade milkshakes but many New Yorkers think they make
the best hamburgers in the city. The ribbed fries
are also hot. When Shake Shack briefly removed
them from the menu, sales dropped.
As a Belgian, I take exception to ribbed fries, but
be my guest and judge for yourself.

FüNFACT

On the website (www.shakeshack.com), under 'locations'
and Madison Square Park, check out THE SHACK CAM.
This live-streaming camera shows how long the line is.

MOVIE TIME

FOR THE LITTLE ONES:

THE SMURFS:
Fans will undoubtedly recognize Belvedere Castle in Central Park from the movie because this is where the Smurfs fought Gargamel. The castle is located in the Park at 79th Street.

MADAGASCAR:
Marty the zebra, Alex the lion, Gloria the hippopotamus and Melman the giraffe live in Central Park Zoo. They're bored and escape to Grand Central Terminal where they get caught and are put on a ship to who knows where...

CLASSICS FOR ALL AGES:

ANNIE (2014):
Many New York buildings are visible in this movie about the well-known orphan, such as the Guggenheim, 4 World Trade Center (Will Stack's apartment), and Beacon Theater. The Italian restaurant where Annie waits for her parents every Friday is Domani, which is 'tomorrow' in Italian, like the famous song (W 4th St. and W 12th St.).

ENCHANTED:
While Giselle waits for her prince, she wanders through the streets of New York. You'll definitely recognize Times Square, Central Park, and Columbus Circle (W 59th St. and Central Park West).

FOR THE ADVENTUROUS:

KING KONG:
In this movie's most famous scene, King Kong climbs the Empire State Building.

SPIDER-MAN (2002):
New York lovers will have a ball with Spider-Man. Flatiron Building, New York Public Library (Bryant Park), Rockefeller Roof Gardens, Roosevelt Island Tramway, Columbia University, and more are portrayed in all their glory.

A TIP FROM PATRICK
Want to see a real movie crew in action? Or maybe bump into a movie star? Keep your eyes wide open. Places where shooting will soon start are indicated by pink, green, or yellow signs.

UNICORN IS THE NEW BLACK

Unicorns have never been so popular, even extending to unicorn companies: these are startups worth at least 1 billion dollars. Think Uber, Snapchat, and Pinterest. Maybe a 'unicorn latte' or an 'explosion cake' with rainbows coming out of it could inspire you to start a company that will one day be worth more than a billion. Still waiting for inspiration? Put on your unicorn horn and have a good time.

FLOUR SHOP

177 Lafayette St., between Broome St. and Grand St., SoHo
www.flourshop.com
Mo.-Th. 11 a.m.-7:30 p.m., Fr.-Su. 11 a.m.-8 p.m., Su. noon-7 p.m.

A cake shop for anyone who loves rainbows and sweets. Flour Shop's only goal is to make you happy. When you cut the cake you are covered in rainbow sprinkles and gumballs. Who wouldn't be happy with that?

BROOKLYN OWL

252 Flatbush Ave., Prospect Heights, Brooklyn
www.brooklynowl.com
718-737-7017
Mo.-Th. 10 a.m.-6 p.m., Fr.-Sa. 10 a.m.-7 p.m., Su. noon-5 p.m.

Ever been on a magical unicorn adventure? Give it a try at the only unicorn store in the world. If you need a horn or some unicorn snot (why not?), this is the place to stock up.

THE END BROOKLYN

522 Metropolitan Ave., between Union St. and Lorimer St., Williamsburg, Brooklyn
thendbrooklyn.com
+1 347-987-3954
Mo.-Su. 8 a.m.-7 p.m.

The term 'unicorn latte' is a bit misleading because there's no espresso in this drink. It's made with living blue or green algae, cold lemon tonic mixed with wildflower and cayenne honey, vanilla pods, and coconut milk. Add some pomegranate, goji powder, and some (sustainable) decorations and it's ready. Definitely worth trying even if it's only for the impressive photo you can take of it.

TAIYAKI

119 Baxter St., between Canal St. and Hester St., Chinatown
www.taiyakinyc.com
+1 212-966-2882
Mo.-Fr. noon-10 p.m., Sa. 11 a.m.-11 p.m., Su. 11 a.m.-10 p.m.

Taiyaki is known for its fish-shaped ice cream cones. Not special enough? Don't worry. Dip into the 'unicorn float.' This is a milkshake with a free unicorn swimming-armband. Perfect for cooling down during those hot New York summer days.

FROM DOWN UNDER TO HIGH ABOVE, LET'S TAKE OFF!

(6-9 YEARS)

3

ROLLING AROUND

ROLLING AROUND

6-9 YEARS   **+/- 3.8 MILES**

MIDTOWN – LONG ISLAND CITY, QUEENS – ROOSEVELT ISLAND – UPPER EAST SIDE

PART I

1. ELLEN'S STARDUST DINER
2. JUNIOR'S
3. TIMES SQUARE
4. DISNEY STORE
5. GULLIVER'S GATE
6. HARD ROCK CAFE
7. MIDTOWN COMICS
8. LA COLOMBE COFFEE ROASTERS
9. KINOKUNIYA
10. WHOLE FOODS MARKET
11. BRYANT PARK
12. NEW YORK PUBLIC LIBRARY – STEPHEN A. SCHWARZMAN BUILDING
13. FIFTH AVENUE: THE DIVIDER
14. LIBRARY WAY
15. GRAND CENTRAL TERMINAL
16. URBAN SPACE
17. CHRYSLER BUILDING
18. 7 TRAIN

SEE NEXT PAGE → → →

ROLLING AROUND

6-9 YEARS **+/- 3.8 MILES**

MIDTOWN – LONG ISLAND CITY,
QUEENS – ROOSEVELT ISLAND –
UPPER EAST SIDE

<u>PART 2</u>

1. COURT SQUARE DINER
2. MOMA PS1
3. COMMUNITEA
4. LIC COMMUNITY BOATHOUSE
5. ROCKAWAY BREWING COMPANY
6. SWEETLEAF
7. PEPSI-COLA SIGN
8. GANTRY PLAZA STATE PARK -
   RAINBOW PLAYGROUND
9. LIC LANDING - COFFEED
10. FERRY TO ROOSEVELT ISLAND
11. ROOSEVELT ISLAND
12. CORNELL TECH
13. FRANKLIN D. ROOSEVELT FOUR FREEDOMS PARK
14. CHERRY BLOSSOM
15. ROOSEVELT ISLAND TRAMWAY
16. BON VIVANT
17. SERENDIPITY 3
18. DYLAN'S CANDYBAR
19. BLOOMINGDALE'S

My way or the highway! Or how about the subway? And the ferry and the cable car. This walk takes you to the nicest park in New York, a garden with a wonderful view of the skyline, and an island that even some New Yorkers forget exists. The route is adventurous but fortunately there are enough spots on the way to recuperate. The path goes from Times Square to Grand Central and, from there, under the water to cool and colorful Queens. Then you can take the boat to Four Freedoms Park and finish off at fancy Bloomingdales via the cable car. Let's hit the road! Or subway...

PART I

❶ ELLEN'S STARDUST DINER
1650 Broadway
www.ellensstardustdiner.com
+1 212-956-5151
🕐 Mo.-Su. 7 a.m.-midnight

A great place to start the day. Maybe not the best breakfast but definitely the most festive. You can eat bacon and eggs here while future Broadway stars bring you coffee, occasionally accompanied by a performance. Want to bet you'll leave this place dancing before you continue the promenade?

❷ JUNIOR'S
Broadway and 49th St.
www.juniorscheesecake.com
🕐 Mo.-Fr. 6:30 a.m.-midnight, Sa.-Su. 6 a.m.-1 a.m.

And the winner is... cheesecake by Junior's. Sis-boom-bah! Believe me, my wife, Ineke, has conducted professional and extensive research into New York's favorite dessert. But do bear in mind that, after one helping, you won't be able to eat another bite for days.

❸ TIMES SQUARE
Broadway, 7th Ave., between 42nd and 47th St.
www.timessquarenyc.org

You either love it or you hate it but you haven't been to New York if you haven't experienced Times Square. If only to give Elmo a hug or take a selfie with the Naked Cowboy. Or to shiver in the freezing cold with 100,000 other deranged tourists waiting on New Year's Eve for the ball on One Times Square to drop.

FUN FACT
The name Times Square comes from the former headquarters of The New York Times.

FUN FACT
Every day about 300,000 pedestrians traverse Times Square.

❹ DISNEY STORE
1540 Broadway and W 46th St., on Times Square
stores.shopdisney.com
+1 212-626-2910
🕐 Mo.-Su. 8 a.m.-1 a.m.

The opening of the door in the morning isn't the only magical moment; overall, a visit to the store feels like a trip to Disneyland. After the rough 70s and 80s when Times Square was a dangerous slum, Disney was the first to venture into setting up a family store here. It was a hit too and now all of Times Square has become one big amusement park. And not just for children either!

⑤ GULLIVER'S GATE

216 W 44th St.

gulliversgate.com

+1 212-235-2016

🕐 Mo.-Su. 10 a.m.-8 p.m.,
$22-$36 a ticket (cheaper online),
0-5 years free.

Not enough time to visit all of New York's neighborhoods? You can see them at this amazing miniature world. A trip to Latin America, the Middle East, or Europe is also possible. Times Square really is the crossroads of the world.

⑥ HARD ROCK CAFE

1501 Broadway and W 43rd St.

www.hardrock.com

+1 212-343-3355

🕐 Su.-Mo. 8 a.m.-1 a.m., Tu.-Th. 9 a.m.-1 a.m., Fr. 9 a.m.-1:30 a.m., Sa. 8 a.m.-1:30 a.m.

This used to be the Paramount Theater, so when you walk in you are also walking into history. Frank Sinatra charmed the public at this theater and in 1964 The Beatles gave a legendary concert here. The set list is still circulating on the internet. This is also the place to get your genuine Hard Rock Cafe New York T-shirt.

⑦ MIDTOWN COMICS

200 W 40th St.

www.midtowncomics.com

+1 212-302-8192

🕐 Mo.-Sa. 8 a.m.-midnight, Su. noon-8 p.m.

One of New York's best comic book stores, with an extensive catalog. Ideal for scoring a couple of rare books or for buying some comics to keep you occupied while waiting in line elsewhere. If you're taking this walk with a young Batman or Spider-Man in tow, you've got to bring them in here.

⑧ LA COLOMBE COFFEE ROASTERS

1045 6th Ave.

www.lacolombe.com

+1 917-386-0157

🕐 Mo.-Fr. 7 a.m.-8 p.m., Sa.-Su. 8 a.m.-8 p.m.

Times when coffee had to be piping hot are behind us. Cold coffee is all the rage in New York even if it isn't in the nineties outside. At La Colombe they even have cold brew on tap. Great for a bout of jetlag.

⑨ KINOKUNIYA

1073 6th Ave., between W 41st and W 42nd St.

usa.kinokuniya.com

+1 (212) 869-1700

🕐 Mo.-Sa. 10 a.m.-8 p.m.

This elegant bookstore has a fine selection of city guides, children's books, graphic novels, art books and novels. Don't be too surprised to find this book there too. Also, don't forget to take the stairs to the basement where they stock a variety of Japanese knick-knacks and books.

⑩ WHOLE FOODS MARKET

1095 6th Ave., between W 41st and W 42nd St.

www.wholefoodsmarket.com

+1 917-728-5700

🕐 Mo.-Su. 7 a.m.-11 p.m.

A good place to get some food and recharge your batteries. This organic supermarket is totally New York, reason enough for a visit. Watch New Yorkers having their vegetables cut for them so they won't have to do it themselves. You can get boxed lunches at the buffet and enjoy them in Bryant Park.

⑪ BRYANT PARK

Between W 40th and W 42nd St. and 5th and 6th Aves.

www.bryantpark.org

🕐 Mo.-Fr. 7 a.m.-midnight, Sa.-Su. 7 a.m.-11 p.m.

This is one of the most charming and lively parks in New York. From juggling acts to ping-pong contests and from ice-skating in the winter to a film festival in the summer; there's something for everyone at

Bryant Park. The nostalgic merry-go-round is recommended ($3 a ride).

You can literally recharge your batteries here: lounge around to your heart's content while your smartphone juices up.

⑫ NEW YORK PUBLIC LIBRARY – STEPHEN A. SCHWARZMAN BUILDING

476 5th Ave.
www.nypl.org
+1 917-275-6975
🕐 Mo. 10 a.m.-5:45 p.m., Tu.-We. 10 a.m.-7:45 p.m., Th.-Sa. 10 a.m.-5:45 p.m., Su. 13 p.m.-5 p.m.

Two marble lions watch over the collection of almost 53 million books and other items. This makes the NYPL the second largest library in the United States and the third largest in the world. Make sure to visit The Rose Main Reading Room and the Children's Center on the ground floor in Room 84. This building has been featured in many shows and movies, including *Seinfeld*, *Sex and the City*, and *Ghostbusters*.

⑬ FIFTH AVENUE: THE DIVIDER

Time to cross the line. Fifth Avenue is more than a world famous shopping street, it also divides Manhattan into East and West. The streets are numbered 0 to 220 and all have an east and a west side. This helps you know which side of Fifth Avenue you are on. It can't get easier than that, but pay attention on Broadway because this boulevard goes right through Manhattan and disrupts the perfect New York grid.

⑭ LIBRARY WAY

E 41st St.

Find inspiration on Library Way in the quotes from major authors such as Oscar Wilde, Gertrude Stein, Lewis Carroll, and many more. Did you ever imagine a walk in the city could be a poetic moment of contemplation?

⑮ GRAND CENTRAL TERMINAL

89 E 42nd St.
🕐 Mo.-Su. 5:30 a.m.-2 a.m.

Admire the famous clock, the breathtaking ceiling decorated with the zodiac, and the mysterious whispering gallery. This is more than simply a station where trains come and go, it's also a popular spot for something to eat or drink. There are five restaurants and cocktail bars and another 20 food stalls downstairs. You can shop in the 50 stores spread throughout the station or in the Great Northern Food Hall. In addition to the 650,000 passengers who pass through daily, another 10,000 people who don't have a train to catch come here too.

FUN FACT

The famous ceiling with the zodiac in Grand Central Terminal is actually a 2400 square yard mistake. The universe is depicted upside down, from God's perspective. Apparently the sketches got mixed up and the mistake was never corrected.

FUN FACT

The Whispering Gallery, next to the Oyster Bar, was designed for discreetly passing on whispered messages. If you stand in one corner, you can whisper something to someone standing in the opposite corner and they'll hear you loud and clear.

16 URBAN SPACE

E 45th St. and Vanderbilt Ave.
www.urbanspacenyc.com
+1 646-747-0810
🕐 Mo.-Fr. 6:30 a.m.-9 p.m., Sa.-Su. 9 a.m.-5 p.m.

You won't find any boring dishes in this food market. This is the place to go for Japanese-inspired Mexican, a sushi burrito, or a lobster sandwich. One thing is for sure: you won't be hungry when you leave.

17 CHRYSLER BUILDING

405 Lexington Avenue
This sublime example of Art-Deco was once the tallest building in New York – and in the world – until the Empire State Building stole the title in 1931. It's still the tallest building on the globe completely constructed from bricks (and a steel framework).

18 7 TRAIN

Take the 7 train to Queens. Get off after three stops at Court Square.

PART 2

1 COURT SQUARE DINER

45-30 23rd St., Long Island City, Queens
www.courtsquarediner.com
+1 718-392-1222
🕐 Open 24 hours.

This old-school diner is partly nestled under the subway rails. Get a load of the long counter, the huge cakes, the unlimited coffee, and a menu loaded with fast food classics. 'Burger and a shake? Coming right up!'

2 MOMA PS1

22-25 Jackson Ave.
www.momaps1.org
+1 718-784-2084
🕐 Th.-Mo. noon-6 p.m.

Is the MoMA not modern enough for you? Then visit MoMA PS1. It often houses exhibitions that are interesting for children too, but not always. So it's worth checking before you go.

3 COMMUNITEA

11-18 46th Rd. and 11th St.
718-729-7708
🕐 Mo.-Th. 8 a.m.-7 p.m., Fr. 8 a.m.-9 p.m., Sa.-Su. 9 a.m.-7 p.m.

Got time for coffee among the Long Island City moms? Children are welcome here and Kafia will greet you with cake and hot drinks made with the utmost care.

4 LIC COMMUNITY BOATHOUSE

46-01 5th St.
www.licboathouse.org
+1 631-542-2628

Ever gone kayaking on the East River? It's a unique experience, especially when the setting sun bathes the water and New York's contours in a red glow.

5 ROCKAWAY BREWING COMPANY

46-01 5th St.
www.rockawaybrewco.com
+1 718-482-6528
🕐 Mo.-Su. 5 p.m.-9 p.m., Th. 3 p.m.-9 p.m., Fr. 3 p.m.-10 p.m., Sa. noon-10 p.m., Su. noon-9 p.m.

You can find Rockaway Brewing Company's beer in many a joint in Brooklyn, Queens and Manhattan, but it tastes best at the place where it's lovingly brewed.

6 SWEETLEAF

4615 Center Blvd.
www.sweetleafcoffee.com
+1 347-527-1038
🕐 Mo.-Th. 7 a.m.-midnight, Fr. 7 a.m.-2 a.m., Sa. 8 a.m.-2 a.m., Su. 8 a.m.-midnight.

Need more coffee for the playground? This is where the moms and dads get their caffeine shots beforehand. New York has many coffee bars but Sweetleaf is one of the best.

⑦ PEPSI-COLA SIGN

33-99 48th Ave.

Urban legend has it that this billboard was erected when actress Joan Crawford, the widow of Pepsi Cola CEO Alfred Steele, was turned down by the former Coca-Cola president for residence at River House. By way of revenge, she had a great billboard placed on the other side of the East River so the residents of River House would think about her every day. Since then it has become a well-known landmark. Photogenic too.

⑧ GANTRY PLAZA STATE PARK - RAINBOW PLAYGROUND

Between 46th and 54th Aves., at 47th Ave.

www.parks.ny.gov

+1 718-786-6385

🕐 Mo.-Su. 8 a.m.-10:30 p.m.

Of all the playgrounds in New York this is Marie's absolute favorite. Not only because it's walking distance from our apartment, but also because of the view of the Manhattan skyline. Marie just can't get enough of the three slides and the rope climbing frame.

⑨ LIC LANDING - COFFEED

52-10 Center Blvd.

www.coffeednyc.com

+1 347-706-4696

🕐 Mo.-Su. 7 a.m.-10 p.m.

If you're feeling up to it, you can walk across the whole park all the way up to LIC Landing. Pleasant paths will take you to the next playground. Get a good coffee or a beer at the open-air cafe, Coffeed. This is where Ineke and I were supposed to get married. Unfortunately, it rained cats and dogs that day but the owner was nice enough to open his other nearby cafe for us.

⑩ FERRY TO ROOSEVELT ISLAND

Center Blvd. and 46th Ave.

www.ferry.nyc

From the Pepsi-Cola Sign, take the ferry to Astoria for $2.75. In less than five minutes, you're on Roosevelt Island.

But be aware that the ferry doesn't always leave on time.

⑪ ROOSEVELT ISLAND

Island on the East River, between Manhattan and Queens

🕐 Open 24 hours.

There used to be a jail on Roosevelt Island as well as a psychiatric home for women, and the first smallpox hospital. The latter is now in ruins and could easily feature as a horror movie set. The biggest attraction on the island is Four Freedoms Park, though the cable car leading to it is an attraction in itself.

⑫ CORNELL TECH

2 W Loop Rd.

www.tech.cornell.edu

This shiny new building is where tomorrow's engineers are educated. It is one of the world's most environment-friendly and energy-efficient campuses.

⑬ FRANKLIN D. ROOSEVELT FOUR FREEDOMS PARK

www.fdrfourfreedomspark.org

+1 212-204-8831

🕐 We.-Mo. 9 a.m.-5 p.m.

In his famous 1941 State of the Union address, President Roosevelt proposed the four freedoms: freedom of speech, freedom of worship, freedom from want, and freedom from fear. This park, designed by Louis Kahn, is an ode to Roosevelt and the freedoms he advocated in his speech. It is no coincidence that the park offers a view of the United Nations building.

⑭ CHERRY BLOSSOM

W Loop Rd.

Every year around the end of March or the beginning of April, the Cherry Blossom Festival takes place on Roosevelt Island. Imagine you're in Japan and let yourself be enchanted by the beauty of the blossoming cherry trees. And maybe by the Japanese festivities too.

⑮ ROOSEVELT ISLAND TRAMWAY

www.rioc.ny.gov
Su.-Th. 6 a.m.-2 a.m.
Fr.-Sa. 6 a.m.-3:30 a.m.

For the price of a subway ride ($2.75), you could also take the famous red cable car, which takes you to Manhattan in a matter of minutes. As an added bonus, you get the amazing view of Manhattan, Queens, and the Queensboro Bridge for free. Of course, if you've seen the Spider-Man movie, you already know this aerial tramway well.

⑯ BON VIVANT

231 E 58th St.
www.bonvivantnewyork.com
+1 646-481-4044
Tu.-Fr. 9:30 a.m.-7:30 p.m.,
Sa. 9:30 a.m.-6:30 p.m.

The *petit fours* at Bon Vivant are almost too beautiful to eat. They come in all kinds of sweet pastel shades, topped with flowers. They make good presents too, especially for marzipan lovers.

⑰ SERENDIPITY 3

225 E 60th St., between 2nd and 3rd Aves., Upper East Side
www.serendipity3.com
+1 212-838-3531
Sa.-Th. 10:30 a.m.-midnight,
Fr. 10:30 a.m.-1 a.m.

Their menu is really extensive but it's virtually impossible not to fall for the 'Frrrozen Hot Chocolate'. Reservations are advisable. Many a celebrity has crossed the threshold here and Andy Warhol was a habitué long before he became a prominent artist.

⑱ DYLAN'S CANDYBAR

East 60th St. and 3rd Ave., Upper East Side
www.dylanscandybar.com
+1 646-735-0078
Su.-Th. 10 a.m.-9 p.m.,
Fr.-Sa. 10 a.m.-11 p.m.

As the name suggests, this is a paradise for sweet-lovers. The time capsules are really cool, with candy from the 50s, 60s, 70s, 80s, and 90s. At Dylan's Candybar Café you can sit in a brightly colored cupcake booth and enjoy a healthy (or not-so-healthy) breakfast or lunch.

⑲ BLOOMINGDALE'S

1000 3rd Ave., 59th St. and Lexington Ave.
www.bloomingdales.com
+1 212-705-2000
Mo.-Sa. 10 a.m.-8:30 p.m.,
Su. 10 a.m.-9 p.m.

If you're too tired to go shopping at this shopper's paradise, take the first elevator to the seventh floor, or to be more precise, seventh heaven, where you can try out the beds. But watch out, because that's dangerously close to the eighth floor, where they stock mini Burberry raincoats and cute little Kate Spade dresses. This is where the rich Upper East Side moms go shopping.

LANGUAGES: FRENCH, ENGLISH, AND CHINESE

HOBBIES: PIANO, ACTING, SOCCER

WANTS TO BE: SOCCER PLAYER

SECRET PLACE IN NEW YORK: THE SOCCER FIELD AT PIER 40

FAVORITE FAST FOOD: MAX BRENNER'S PIZZA WITH MARSHMALLOWS

FAVORITE RESTAURANT: NINJA NEW YORK AND MIMI CHENG'S

LIVES IN: CHINATOWN, MANHATTAN

ROMAN CALL ME YOY CHANG LOUAN

I like to take my clients to Williamsburg. One of the coziest and, above all, tastiest places there is Caprices by Sophie. Sophie is a Frenchwoman who makes little meringue pastries in her own small shop. One day when I walked in with my clients, I noticed a mischievous-looking boy doing his homework. He heard me speaking Dutch and immediately asked what language it was. He proudly told me that he speaks French, English, and Chinese. At first I didn't believe him because he didn't look at all Asian. All the more reason for him to bowl me over with a deluge of Chinese sentences. He turned out to be Sophie's son and he'd learned Chinese at school. Roman to his mom and dad, Yoy Chang Louan to his friends.

Roman (7) lives in Chinatown in Manhattan. When it was time to choose a school, the public school in their neighborhood turned out to be the best choice. In his French parents' eyes, the fact that classes are given in both English and Chinese was an added advantage. Roman was just happy that he could be in the same class as his best friend from kindergarten. The rest didn't matter much to him. His parents are also happy with the school. And they don't mind that, for parent-teacher conferences, they need an interpreter to communicate with the Chinese teacher. Pretty soon Roman himself could do the interpreting.

After three years of Chinese, he's already getting pretty fluent. He chats with people on the street and knows exactly who's talking Chinese and whose mother tongue is some other Asian language. When a sushi delivery boy came to the door one day, he immediately started chatting with him. He knew at once that the delivery boy was not Japanese, but Chinese!

After school, this seven-year-old New Yorker still has a busy schedule. Like many other kids here, he has lots of hobbies, which could help him later in his academic career. He plays piano, does jiu-jitsu and has six hours of drama classes on Saturdays. Besides that, he obviously has a lot of homework to do in both English and Chinese and he really likes to play soccer. Roman wants to be a soccer player when he grows up. Maybe he'll end up on a Chinese team.

If Roman still has some free time left, he likes to go to shows like *The Big Apple Circus* and the *Rockettes* in Rockefeller Center, and he likes to play in Tompkins Square Park. He likes to go say hi to the eagle that lives there. He also celebrated his 7th birthday in this park. His little brother, Vadim, has even bigger plans. He wants to celebrate his next birthday at the Empire State Building. You can't start too early on the American Dream.

⊜ TIPS FROM ROMAN

MAX BRENNER CHOCOLATE BAR

841 Broadway, between E 13th St. and E 14th St.,
Greenwich Village
www.maxbrenner.com
+1 646-467-8803
Mo.-Th. 9 a.m.-midnight, Fr.-Sa. 9 a.m.-1 a.m.,
Su. 9 a.m.-11 p.m.

A place where they make pizza with
chocolate and marshmallows. Where
chocolate fondue comes from a tower
and the chocolate shot on the menu is
for anyone who doesn't get high on the
smell of chocolate alone. It's like being
in Willy Wonka's chocolate factory,
only you don't need a golden ticket to
get in. All chocoholics are welcome.

MIMI CHENG'S

179 2nd Ave., between 11th St. and 12th St.,
East Village
+1 212-533-2007
Mo.-Th. 11:30 a.m.-9:30 p.m., Th.-Sa. 11:30 a.m.-
10 p.m., Su. 11:30 a.m.-9:30 p.m.
380 Broom St., between Mott St. and
Mulberry St., Little Italy
+1 212-343-1387
Mo.-Su. 11 a.m.-9:30 p.m.
www.mimichengs.com

This is the place for fresh dumplings
just like in Taiwan. The dumpling
was invented in the 13th century
and is possibly one of the oldest ever
on-the-go dishes, but still good.
Certainly in this dumpling paradise.

 FUN FACT

About half of the population of New York
speaks a second language at home.

 FUN FACT

More Chinese live in New York than in any other city
outside of Asia.

 FUN FACT

More than 800 different languages are spoken
in New York.

NINJA NEW YORK

25 Hudson St., between Duane St. and Read St., TriBeCa
www.ninjanewyork.com
+1 212-274-8500
Mo.-Th. 5:45 p.m.-11 p.m., Fr.-Sa. 4:45 p.m.-11 p.m.,
Su. 4:45 p.m.-10 p.m.

Pow! Whack! Whoosh! The dishes fly through
the air and the waiters bounce off the walls.
It may be a bit over the top, but still: you get
more than just service; you get treated to a real
show. Maybe not the tastiest food in New York
but for sure the neatest experience.

⊜ A TIP FROM INEKE

CAPRICES BY SOPHIE

138 N 6th St., between Berry St. and Bedford Ave.,
Williamsburg, Brooklyn
www.capricesbysophie.com
+1 347-689-4532
Mo.-Su. 8 a.m.-8 p.m.

A *caramel capricieux* or a *croquembouche* or
chouquettes instead? No idea what these words
mean? Just try them out at Caprices by Sophie,
where Roman's mom makes the best cakes in
New York. The menu also includes many gluten-
free treats. You can take a breather in the garden, an oasis of peace in the middle of the bustle
of Williamsburg.

ICE CREAM PARADISE

ODD FELLOWS ICE CREAM CO.

75 Kent Ave., Williamsburg, Brooklyn
75 East 4th St., East Village
379 Suydam St., Bushwick
www.oddfellowsnyc.com
Su.-Th. noon-11 p.m., Fr.-Sa. noon-midnight

When was the last time you ate a scoop of Olive Oil & Blackberry or Buttermilk Apple in a freshly baked sugar cone? Did you say 'never?' This is your chance.

AMPLE HILLS CREAMERY

623 Vanderbilt Ave., Prospect Heights, Brooklyn
Su.-Th. noon-10 p.m., Fr.-Sa. noon-11 p.m.
Gotham West Market, 600 11th Ave., Midtown
Bubby's High Line, 72 Gansevoort St., Meatpacking District
www.amplehills.com
Mo.-Th. noon-10 p.m., Fr. noon-11 p.m., Sa. 11 a.m.-11 p.m.,
Su. 11 a.m.-10 p.m.

This homemade ice cream is a concept in New York. Flavors such as 'Ooey Gooey Butter Cake' and 'The Munchies' are worth a trip to Brooklyn. But since another branch has now opened next to the High Line, Manhattanites don't even need to leave their neighborhood when they have a craving for a scoop of Ample Hills ice cream. But watch out: this ice cream is highly addictive.

TIPSY SCOOP

217 E 26th St., between 2nd and 3rd Ave., Gramercy
www.tipsyscoop.com
+1 917-388-2862
Tu.-We. noon-10 p.m., Th.-Sa. noon-11 p.m.,
Su. noon-6 p.m.

This very first *barlour* (bar + ice cream parlor) serves ice cream with alcohol. All the flavors are based on cocktails and have an alcohol content of about 5%. From 'Maple Bacon Bourbon' to 'Dark Chocolate Whiskey Salted Caramel,' they're all irresistible. Adults only: you must be 21 or older to taste these tipsy scoops.

FUN FACT

It's illegal in New York to carry an ice cream cone in your pocket on Sundays. Not that you're planning to... but there's a funny story to it. Eating ice cream on a Sunday used to be forbidden. New Yorkers who wanted to get around the prohibition hid their ice cream in a large coat pocket. Which explains this wacky law.

LANGUAGES IN NY

176 LANGUAGES ARE SPOKEN IN THE NEW YORK SCHOOLS.
THE NUMBER OF LANGUAGES SPOKEN IN HOMES IS ESTIMATED AT 800.
LINGUISTICALLY SPEAKING, NEW YORK IS THE MOST DIVERSE CITY IN THE WORLD.
IN FOUR OUT OF TEN HOUSEHOLDS ENGLISH IS NOT THE SPOKEN LANGUAGE.

(DO)NUTS IN THE CITY

Every first Friday in June is National Donut Day in the US, when many bakeries hand out free donuts. You have to be crazy not to eat a donut on this day. Grown-ups are also into it. They wear donut t-shirts or donut-shaped earrings. In New York, everybody can let their inner child hang out... but you have to get out of bed early because the donuts could already be sold out by 9 a.m. Many people buy large boxes of them to give to colleagues or friends.

HISTORY OF THE DONUT

The Dutch settlers brought *oliebollen* (literally 'oil balls'–fried balls of dough, usually with raisins) to New York, which back then was still called New Amsterdam. They called them *Olykoeks* or 'oily cakes.' The donut did not become popular until WWI. They were sent to soldiers on the front and new immigrants who had just set foot on Ellis Island were welcomed with a donut. This was literally their first taste of the US. Donuts are now even more popular, since well-known chefs have begun inventing new varieties. For instance, Dominique Ansel invented the 'cronut,' which is a cross between a croissant and a donut. It's been some years since it was launched but, every day, New Yorkers still stand in line to buy one.

THE SHAPE

How come the round *oliebol* was replaced by a donut with a hole in the middle? There are two theories. According to the former, the center of the donut was always a bit raw and the inventor of the donut was Hansen Gregory, an American captain, who had the sticky core taken out. He didn't like his mother's half-baked schemes. The second theory claims that the captain needed both hands to steer the ship. The donut's hole made it possible to prop it on one of the handles during difficult maneuvers.

The donut holes don't go to waste, by the way. If you want a small taste you can buy the punched out centers.

THE NAME

Maybe the name comes from the fact that the center was always raw and that nuts were put into it to improve the flavor. Or it may come from 'dough knots.'

PATRICK'S FAVORITE

SEE MORE ON BE**NY** Minute ▶/BENYMINUTE

DOUGHNUT PLANT

220 W 23rd St., between 7th and 8th Aves., Chelsea
Su.-We. 7 a.m.-10 p.m., Th.-Sa. 7 a.m.-midnight
379 Grand St., between Essex St. and Clinton St., Lower East Side
Su.-Th. 6:30 a.m.-8 p.m., Fr.-Sa. 6:30 a.m.-9 p.m.
www.doughnutplant.com

These donuts are made from natural and organic ingredients. They have yeast donuts, cake donuts, and filled donuts. The square filled donut is great. Not only because of the shape but also (and chiefly) because of the taste.

NYPD FAVORITES: KRISPY KREME AND DUNKIN' DONUTS

Yeah, cops eat lots of donuts. You could say policemen were made of sugar. But the New York police are often very rough; so not much sugar on the inside...

DONUTS FOR CONNOISSEURS: DOMINIQUE ANSEL BAKERY

Tired of the cronut? Dominique Ansel probably has a new creation for you, such as the holiday special, eggnog cronut.

INEKE'S FAVORITE

DOUGH DOUGHNUT

14 W 19th St., between 5th and 6th Aves., Chelsea
Mo.-Th. 6 a.m.-8 p.m., Fr. 6 a.m.-9 p.m., Sa. 7 a.m.-9 p.m., Su. 7 a.m.-8 p.m.
700 8th Ave., between W 44th and W 45th St., Times Square
Mo.-Fr. 6:30 a.m.-9 p.m., Sa.-Su. 9 a.m.-5 p.m.
www.doughdoughnuts.com

These large yeast donuts are handmade. The flavors are unique, such as the hibiscus donut. Available in many coffee houses in the city.

MARIE'S FAVORITE

PETER PAN DONUT & PASTRY SHOP

727 Manhattan Ave., between Meserole Ave. and Norman Ave., Greenpoint, Brooklyn
www.peterpandonuts.com
Mo.-Fr. 4:30 a.m.-8 p.m., Sa. 5 a.m.-8 p.m., Su. 5:30 a.m.-7 p.m.

This small shop is hidden away somewhere in Greenpoint but true donut fans will always find it. It's on all the lists of New York's best donuts. So Marie can also consider becoming a donut critic.

FAVORITE RESTAURANT: BXL ZOUTE FOR THE CHEESE CROQUETTES

FAVORITE STORE: DYLAN'S CANDYBAR

HOBBIES: HIP-HOP, COOKING CLUB

LANGUAGES: DUTCH, ENGLISH

WANTS TO BE: COOK

FAVORITE PLAYGROUND: ADVENTURE PLAYGROUND IN CENTRAL PARK

FAVORITE DAY OF THE YEAR: HALLOWEEN, THIS YEAR DRESSED UP AS FRANKIE STEIN FROM MONSTER HIGH

LIVES IN: UPPER WEST SIDE, MANHATTAN

LEONIE GET THE PARTY STARTED

I have nothing but good memories of my own birthday parties when I was a child. The concept was always simple and it was the same every year. But even so, I was already counting down weeks beforehand. Mom and dad made waffles while my friends and I horsed around and built forts in the garden. I didn't need much more than that. Children's parties in New York are slightly different. With small apartments and no gardens, parties can't be held at home. And of course, there's the inevitable competition between parents to organize the best, biggest, and most expensive birthday party ever. Children's parties are therefore big business in New York.

I got to know Leonie (7) in the Belgian cafe, BXL. Like me, she has Belgian roots and she loves going there with her parents to eat cheese croquettes while I go to drink Belgian beer. When we meet, she often tells me about the latest extravagant birthday parties she's been invited to. As an entertainer, Leonie is very popular among her classmates and therefore a favorite invitee on the New York children's birthday party scene.

It looks like the motto is 'the more spectacular and the more expensive, the better.' Leonie knows all about it. She told me about a party in which everybody became a real model. All the kids got a makeover: their hair was done, they were made up, and they had a manicure. And after they were decked out in the latest fashions, they could strut on a real catwalk to the constant flashing of a professional photographer's camera.

Kamil's seventh (!) birthday party took place in a nightclub. Everyone was covered in neon tape so they could glow in the dark. And then the dancing started. A robot showed them the moves. Three guesses where Kamil will celebrate his 21st birthday...
Happily there are also children who 'just' organize their parties in a playground. But not without a clown who makes balloon animals and a professional makeup artist who paints the most beautiful fairy-tale characters on those cute little faces. Another permanent fixture is a mountain of cupcakes decorated with the birthday boy's or girl's name.

It shouldn't be too long before Leonie is baking her own cupcakes for her birthday parties: she goes to cooking classes and has also taken cooking lessons at Sur La Table and Williams Sonoma, two classy kitchenware companies that also offer workshops. I've had the pleasure of trying some of Leonie's delicious gingerbread cookies and an ice cream sundae. Time to send Marie to cooking classes too and start saving money for her parties.

COOKING CLASSES FOR CHILDREN

SUR LA TABLE COOKING LESSONS
www.surlatable.com

JUNIOR CHEF COOKING CLASSES AT WILLIAMS SONOMA
www.williams-sonoma.com

PARTY IN THE CITY

Is it your birthday while you're in New York? Make sure to take a look in Party City. They sell streamers and decorations for every possible theme; from Finding Dory to Super Mario. They also have the neatest balloons (including ones for every letter of the alphabet) and, if you like, they'll blow them up for you too. No one will be surprised if you go into the subway with your whole name spelled in balloons. Just avoid the revolving doors; I've seen many a birthday kid get stuck.

If you go out to eat, let them know it's your birthday. You'll often get a free dessert or they'll sing *Happy Birthday* at your table. That'll surely double your birthday feeling.

PARTY CITY
Several locations in the city:
www.partycity.com

A TIP FROM MARIE

Always wear a crown or a party hat when it's your birthday. You won't believe how many people will congratulate you.

⊜ A TIP FROM LEONIE

BXL ZOUTE
50 W 22nd St., between 5th and 6th Aves., Flatiron District
www.bxlrestaurants.com
+1 646-692-9282
Mo.-Fr. 11:30 a.m.-11:30 p.m., Sa. 11 a.m.-11:30 p.m.
Want to help European supporters cheer for their favorite soccer team? Or how about tasting a Belgian vol-au-vent or beef stew with a Belgian beer? Belgians like to come to this restaurant to meet friends or for a taste of home.

FUN FACT

The first brewery in the United States was founded by – who else? – the Belgian who bought Manhattan: Peter Minuit.

I WANT CANDY

ECONOMY CANDY

108 Rivington St., between Ludlow St. and Essex St., Little Italy

www.economycandy.com

+1 212-254-1531

Mo. 10 a.m.-6 p.m., Tu.-Fr. 9 a.m.-6 p.m., Sa. 10 a.m.-6 p.m., Su. 9 a.m.-6 p.m.

With more than 2000 kinds of candy to choose from, this is a true New York icon. The candy from your childhood days that you can no longer find anywhere else? *Satellite Wafers, Wax Lips* or *Absinthe Mints*? Good chance they'll have them here.

BON BON

130 Allen St.

www.bonbonnyc.myshopify.com

+1 212-786-0094

Mo.-Su. 10 a.m.-10 p.m.

Acute case of candy craving? Bon Bon will get you through: this is the first candy store that delivers. All the sweets at this Swedish candy store are made without saturated fats or genetically modified organisms and all the colorings are natural. This is your big chance to let your children eat sweets without feeling like a bad parent. Until you remember that they do contain sugar, of course... and not just a tiny bit either.

DYLAN'S CANDYBAR

East 60th St. and 3rd Ave.

Su.-Th. 10 a.m.-9 p.m., Fr.-Sa. 10 a.m.-11 p.m.

33 Union Square

Mo.-Th. 11 a.m.-10 p.m., Fr. 11 a.m.-11 p.m., Sa. 10 a.m.-11 p.m., Su. 11 a.m.-9 p.m.

www.dylanscandybar.com

Ralph Lauren's daughter has created a paradise for all lovers of sweet things. Candy is everywhere, even in the ground. Want to know the favorite candy of some famous New Yorkers, usually Papa Ralph's friends? Then go see the basement.

M&M'S WORLD

1600 Broadway and W 48th St., Times Square

www.mmsworld.com

+1 212-295-3850

Mo.-Su. 9 a.m.-midnight

Do you like only red or blue M&M's? This is the place to buy your favorite color. But the best part is that you can get a hug from a giant 'real' M&M. Cameras ready? Set... Pose...

EATING OUT

My experience with Marie is that she's much calmer in the more chic restaurants. In the so-called child-friendly establishments, the commotion automatically gets to her, making it harder for her to stay put, because there's so much to see and do. And to top it off, the food there is usually less tasty.

We go out to eat with Marie several times a week. It costs about the same as cooking at home and we're usually far from home after a tour or an urban safari.

Usually we give Marie some bread and water first (in a sippy cup with a straw). Don't be afraid to ask for one too. While she eats her bread we have time to read the menu.

Don't be embarrassed! Just ask them to hold anything your child doesn't like from a dish. Being difficult when ordering is common practice in New York, so they won't be taken aback. And if they know it's for a child they'll do their best for you.

How's this for an example: '*I'll have the quinoa salad, make sure there are no nuts and no tomatoes but extra carrots in it. Go light on the dressing and oh, egg whites only...*' It may seem like a sitcom scene but it's nothing out of the ordinary in New York.
Always bring toys along. Stickers, books, and finger puppets are ideal.

3 TIPS FOR DIFFICULT EATERS:

- Check the menu online beforehand
  to find out what the options are.
- In a bodega or the Prepared Foods
  department at Whole Foods or one
  of the other quality supermarkets,
  it's easy to choose because you can
  point to what you want.
- Bring your own snacks. This
  usually isn't a problem. Not ordering from the children's menu is also
  acceptable. Just order something
  from the adult menu and ask for a
  smaller portion.

ALL-AMERICAN RESTAURANTS

JUNIOR'S RESTAURANT AND BAKERY
1515 Broadway and 45th St., Times Square
www.juniorscheesecake.com
+1 212-302-2000
Mo.-Fr. 6:30 a.m.-midnight, Sa.-Su. 6 a.m.-1 a.m.
Junior's has a large selection of
dishes but people actually come for
the cheesecake, a New York specialty
for which the city is well known.
Of all the bakeries, Junior's makes
the best cheesecake, in Ineke's
opinion. Believe me, she's done plenty
of research.

AMERICAN GIRL CAFE
75 Rockefeller Plaza, Midtown
www.americangirl.com/retail/new_york_city.php
+1 877-247-5223
Mo.-Th. 11 a.m.-1:30 p.m., Fr. 11 a.m.-5:30 p.m.,
Sa. 9:30 a.m.-7 p.m., Su. 9:30 a.m.-5 p.m.
Taking a doll along on the trip? She will get her
own seat at the table and even her own plate to
'eat' from. A great experience for every doll fan.
Don't forget to reserve.

SWEET CHICK
178 Ludlow St., between E Houston St. and Stanton St., NoLIta
164 Bedford Ave. and N 8th St., Williamsburg, Brooklyn
www.sweetchick.com
Mo.-Fr. 11 a.m.-2 a.m., Sa.-Su. 10 a.m.-2 a.m.
Waffles with chicken. It may sound disgusting
but it's worth trying. And Sweet Chick is a good
place too.

HAPPY & HEALTHY

New Yorkers unhealthy? No way! Research started by Michael Bloomberg, the former mayor of New York City, concluded that there is a direct correlation between unhealthy eating habits and poverty. You could probably guess that in the rich neighborhoods there's a plethora of healthy food and beverage establishments. Here's a list of our favorites.

TAKUMEN

5-50 50th Ave. between Vernon Blvd. and 5th St.,
LIC, Queens
www.takumenlic.com
+1 718-361-7973
Tu.-Fr. 8 a.m.-10:30 p.m., Sa.-Su. 10 a.m.-10:30 p.m.
Takumen is so good you might consider moving to Long Island City just so you can eat there every week. And that's exactly what I did. Besides the scrumptious *ramen* and rice dishes, they also have delicious Parlor coffee for me, matcha latte for Ineke and Morgenstern's ice cream for Marie. A guaranteed success.

DR SMOOD

485 Lexington Ave.
www.drsmood.com
+1 786-334-4420
Mo.-Fr. 7 a.m.-8 p.m., Sa. 9 a.m.-6 p.m.
Smart food for a good mood. Dr Smood has a keen eye for detail. Not only in the dishes but also when it comes to the choice of music and the interior. This is a delectable oasis of calm coziness.

ROSEMARY'S

18 Greenwich Ave. and W 10th St., Greenwich Village
www.rosemarysnyc.com
+1 212-647-1818
Mo.-Fr. 10 a.m.-11 p.m., Sa.-Su. 10 a.m.-4 p.m. and 15 p.m.-11 p.m.
Italian restaurant with a garden on the roof where they grow vegetables and herbs. They have a special (and healthy) children's menu and delicious cookies for dessert.

IN A NEW Y
EVERYTHIN
CHANGE

RK MINUTE, CAN

DON HENLEY IN THE SONG
NEW YORK MINUTE

WANTS TO BE: <u>DOCTOR</u>

HOBBIES: <u>DANCING, TENNIS, CLIMBING, CRAFTS</u>

LANGUAGES: <u>DUTCH, ENGLISH, SPANISH</u>

FAVORITE ICE CREAM: <u>MISTER SOFTIE, ICE CREAM WITH RAINBOW SPRINKLES</u>

FAVORITE PLACE IN NEW YORK: <u>CONEY ISLAND AND GOVERNORS ISLAND</u>

FAVORITE MUSEUM: <u>GUGGENHEIM</u>

FAVORITE SNACK: <u>HOT DOG</u>

FAVORITE FOOD: <u>SUSHI AND SPAGHETTI AND MEATBALLS</u>

LIVES IN: <u>DOWNTOWN BROOKLYN</u>

FELICE   IN A NEW YORK MINUTE

In New York time goes faster than anywhere else in the world. In just a few seconds magical things can happen, which explains the term 'New York minute.' One time when I was in Grand Central Terminal I heard a Dutch woman say to her mother: 'If that guy with the yellow jacket would move out of the way I'd at least be able to take a selfie.' She didn't realize that of the 650,000 people who pass through the station every day, there could also be someone who speaks her own language. I happily obliged by taking their picture and in the short conversation we had I got to know Marie Cecile and her mother.

Marie Cecile and her husband and two children moved to New York from the Netherlands. We kept in touch through Facebook and became good virtual friends, as we never actually met in person. Until I sent a message asking whether I could interview Felice (8) and Colin (6) for this book. Bingo.

I love following Colin's and Felice's adventures via Facebook. The siblings were born in Philadelphia, were adopted in the Netherlands, and moved to New York four years ago because of their father's work. Life can be so unpredictable. Colin and Felice love growing up in their country of birth. In the meantime, Felice has become a true local. She gets around on her scooter, likes to eat sushi, and on weekends she mostly likes to attend a high tea. She also likes to take the boat to Governors Island where there are many playgrounds to enjoy on a Sunday afternoon. Her brother, Colin, has also adjusted well to his new hometown. He knows all the basketball courts in Brooklyn Heights and when he gets hungry from playing so much, the thing he likes to eat most is a Nathan's or Gray's Papaya hot dog. The real thing.

⊜ A TIP FROM FELICE

YÙNHÓNG CHOPSTICKS
50 Mott St., Chinatown
Mo.-Su. 10:30 a.m.-8:30 p.m.
This shop sells single chopsticks.
They have unique hand-painted
specimens and special sticks for
teaching children how to eat with
them. Because you can never start too
early, of course. That is, if you want to
impress grandpa and grandma or the
Chinese restaurant around the corner.

HAVE FUN ON CONEY ISLAND

Subway lines D, F, N and Q all end at Coney Island, famous for its fantastic amusement
parks, strolls along the boardwalk and the view of the Atlantic from the beach. You could
actually call it the city's entertainment hub–but a magnified version. Every 4th of July
there's a hot dog eating contest, when the contestants stuff themselves full in seconds.
Just imagine yourself in magical underwater worlds as you watch the Mermaid Parade.
In July and August, there are fireworks every Friday at 9:30 p.m. The best place to watch
the show is from the boardwalk or the beach between W 10th St. and W 15th St.

LUNA PARK ON CONEY ISLAND
1000 Surf Ave., Brooklyn
www.lunaparknyc.com
Variable opening hours.

Three amusement parks were constructed on Coney Island between 1895 and 1904. Some of the attractions are so unique that they are now protected and may never be dismantled. For instance, the famous Wonder Wheel, The Cyclone, one of the world's oldest, still-working wooden rollercoasters, and Parachute Jump. The latter is no longer in use but is often called the Eiffel Tower of Coney Island because its silhouette is easily recognizable from afar.

FUN FACT
Lola Glass, a nine-year-old artist, has already created several graffiti murals. This young talent has covered walls at Bushwick Collective and Deno's Wonder Wheel Amusement Park on Coney Island. She's often called the world's youngest graffiti artist. (@lolatheillustrator on Instagram)

FUN FACT
At the beginning of the 18th century, premature babies were exhibited on the boardwalk. It may sound sinister but it was well-intended. Visitors had to pay a quarter to see the poor creatures. Doctor Martin Couney collected the money to help care for the babies.

MERMAID PARADE
Coney Island
www.coneyisland.com/programs/mermaid-parade

The Mermaid Parade is always on the Saturday closest to June 21. The parade celebrates the start of the summer swimming season. Several thousand people in costume participate in the parade. Even children and dogs participate or come to watch, though the Coney Island website does warn parents that mermaids and mer-men – let's face it – are often scantily dressed, with only a couple of strategically positioned starfish. Not everyone wants their children to witness the minimalistic costumes.

A TIP FROM PATRICK
Join the Coney Island Polar Bear New Year's Day Plunge. Every January 1, hundreds of courageous 'polar bears' brave the icy water to get the year off to a freezing start. Beware! It can be really cold. I speak from experience...

FUN FACT
The Dutch called the island *Conyne Eylandt* or *Konijneneiland* (both mean Rabbit Island). Through Anglicization, it later became Coney Island.

4TH OF JULY: HOT DOG EATING CONTEST

On Independence Day in 1916, four immigrants held a hot dog eating contest. This was their way of testing which of them was the most patriotic. The contest has now grown into an annual event. The rules are simple: eat as many hot dogs as possible in ten minutes. In 2018, the winner, Joey Chestnut, ate 74 hot dogs. That's more than seven a minute or about 8.1 seconds per hot dog. So it's more about stuffing than eating. Gobble down, gobble up.

FELTMAN'S VERSUS NATHAN'S

The hot dog was invented 150 years ago by the German immigrant Charles Feltman. He put a sausage into a specially designed elongated bun and called it a 'red hot.' His invention was an immediate success. About fifty years later, Nathan Handwerker came to work for Feltman as a bun cutter. Soon afterwards Nathan started his own company. His hot dogs were 5 cents cheaper. Nathan's survived the depression but Feltman's went bankrupt.

Now, almost one hundred years later, Feltman's has reopened in the Luna Park, around the corner from Nathan's. So the competition can start again.

FELTMAN'S
1000 Surf Ave., Brooklyn
80 Saint Mark's Place, Manhattan
www.feltmansofconeyisland.com

NATHAN'S
1310 Surf Ave., Coney Island, Brooklyn
Stalls all over Manhattan
www.nathansfamous.com
Su.-Th. 9 a.m.-11 p.m., Fr.-Sa. 9 a.m.-midnight

HOT DOGS IN MANHATTAN

DANISH DOGS BY CLAUS MEYER
87 E 42nd St., Grand Central Terminal, Midtown
www.greatnorthernfood.com
Mo.-Fr. 6 a.m.-10 p.m., Sa.-Su. 8 a.m.-9 p.m.
It's a New York tradition to take a
simple classic dish and turn it into a
connoisseur's specialty. Claus Meyer
devised this gourmet hot dog, otherwise known as the Danish dog.
In the morning they serve delicious
egg sandwiches; the perfect way to
start the day. Since you're already
here, go take a look in Grand Central's
Great Northern Food Hall.

PAPAYA KING VERSUS GRAY'S PAPAYA

Not the obvious names for hot dog joints,
but they're often declared New York's best.
The name comes from the fruit drinks they
serve with the hot dogs, such as grape juice, piña
colada and coconut champagne–all alcohol-free.
Since the very first Papaya King opened in a
German neighborhood, the owner decided to sell
hot dogs as well. Eventually his hot dogs became
more famous than his fruit juices, although
connoisseurs consider them a perfect pairing.
Gray's Papaya is actually copied from the original Papaya King but most people say his hot dogs
are better.

PAPAYA KING

179 E 86th St., Upper East Side
www.papayaking.com
Su.-Th. 8 a.m.-midnight, Fr.-Sa. 8 a.m.-1 a.m.

GRAY'S PAPAYA

2090 Broadway and 72nd St., Upper West Side
612 8th Ave., between W 39th and W 40th St., Times Square
www.grayspapayanyc.com
Open 24 hours.

NATHAN'S HOT DOG EATING CONTEST

IN 2018, JOEY CHESTNUT WON NATHAN'S HOT DOG EATING CON-
TEST FOR THE ELEVENTH TIME BY DOWNING 74 HOT DOGS
IN TEN MINUTES. CAN ANYONE BEAT THAT?

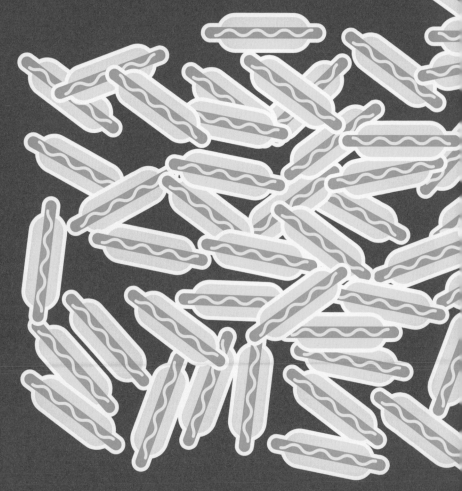

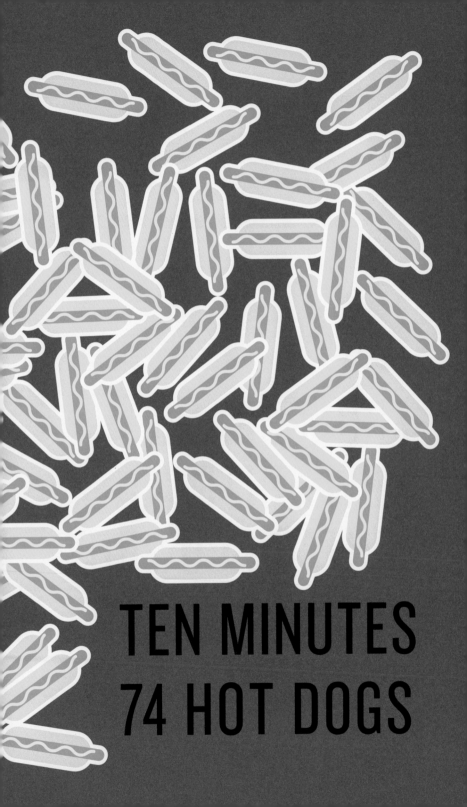

TEN MINUTES
74 HOT DOGS

FROM BRAND NEW SUITS TO VINTAGE COWBOY BOOTS

(9-12 YEARS)

JUMPING
AROUND

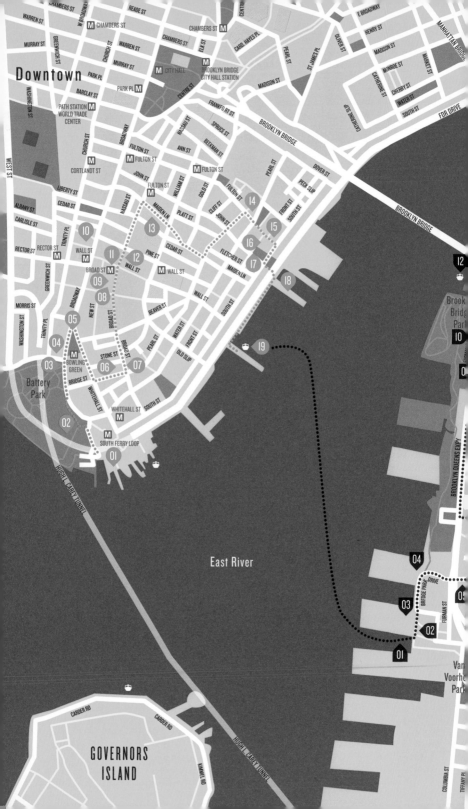

JUMPING AROUND

9-12 YEARS **+/- 4.5 MILES**

FINANCIAL DISTRICT –
SOUTH STREET SEAPORT –
BROOKLYN HEIGHTS – DUMBO

PART I: BRAND-NEW SUITS

1. STATEN ISLAND FERRY
2. SEAGLASS CAROUSEL
3. NETHERLAND MONUMENT
4. BROADWAY
5. CHARGING BULL
6. CAFE GRUMPY
7. STONE STREET
8. NEW YORK STOCK EXCHANGE
9. FEARLESS GIRL
10. TRINITY CHURCH
11. WALL STREET
12. FEDERAL HALL
13. FEDERAL RESERVE BANK OF NEW YORK
14. PEARL STREET PLAYGROUND
15. IPIC THEATERS
16. SOUTH STREET SEAPORT MUSEUM
17. IMAGINATION PLAYGROUND
18. PIER 15
19. NY WATERWAY

SEE NEXT PAGE → → →

JUMPING AROUND

9-12 YEARS   +/- 4.5 MILES

FINANCIAL DISTRICT –
SOUTH STREET SEAPORT –
BROOKLYN HEIGHTS – DUMBO

PART 2: VINTAGE COWBOY BOOTS

1 FERRY BROOKLYN BRIDGE PARK /
   ATLANTIC AVENUE STOP
2 WATER LAB & SLIDE PARADISE & SWING VALLEY
3 BROOKLYN BRIDGE PARK - PIER 6 -
   BEACH VOLLEYBALL COURTS
4 PICNIC PENINSULA PLAYGROUND
5 JORALEMON STREET
6 HÄAGEN-DAZS ICE CREAM SHOP
7 BROOKLYN HEIGHTS PROMENADE
8 70 WILLOW STREET
9 PEDESTRIAN BRIDGE TO PROMENADE
10 1 HOTEL BROOKLYN BRIDGE
11 BROOKLYN ICE CREAM FACTORY
12 THE RIVER CAFÉ
13 JULIANA'S
14 GRIMALDI'S
15 ST. ANN'S WAREHOUSE
16 JANE'S CAROUSEL
17 BROOKLYN HISTORICAL SOCIETY
18 FEED SHOP & CAFE
19 CECCONI'S
20 PEBBLE BEACH
21 PERFECT PICTURE – EMPIRE STATE BUILDING
   UNDER THE MANHATTAN BRIDGE
22 GLEASON'S GYM
23 BROOKLYN ROASTING COMPANY
24 SUBWAY F TRAIN

Walking through the streets of New Amsterdam (New York, in the year 1625), discover yesteryear's downtown as well as today's. Are you searching for gold or searching for happiness? The gold here is deep underground as well as high in the skyscrapers, and sometimes even in the streets.

After crossing Manhattan, we take the boat to Brooklyn. Be careful, because the view will make you want to jump up and down. Visit the amazing playgrounds, beach volleyball courts, and merry-go-rounds surrounded by Brooklyn's cool cats. If you get tired, plop down in a park, a cafe, or a coffee bar.

PART 1: BRAND-NEW SUITS

STATEN ISLAND FERRY

4 Whitehall St.
www.siferry.com
+1 212-639-9675
Open 24 hours

The ferry sails from Manhattan to Staten Island and takes 25 minutes. It's a magnificent cruise, not only for Staten Island's inhabitants but also for tourists. During the crossing, you get a great free view of the Statue of Liberty. The ferry sails day and night, every half hour. There's not much to see in this borough so the best thing to do is to take the same ferry back and wave again to the iconic statue.

❷ SEAGLASS CAROUSEL

State St. & Water St.

🕐 Su.-Th. 10 a.m.-7 p.m., Fr.-Sa. 10 a.m.-8 p.m.

You could go for a couple of rounds on this stunning merry-go-round. It's almost as if you're diving among the East River fish.

❸ NETHERLAND MONUMENT

Bowling Green and Broadway

www.nycgovparks.org/parks/battery-park/monuments/1092

The Netherlands made a gift of this monument to commemorate the purchase of Manhattan. The island was discovered in 1609 by Henry Hudson and bought from the Native Americans by the Belgian Peter Minuit for 60 guilders (about $1000 in today's money). This has got to be the best deal ever made!

❹ BROADWAY

On hearing the word Broadway, everyone thinks of musicals. But it really is a broad way. It's a street that crosses all of Manhattan and even stretches all the way to the Bronx. Since Broadway already existed when the city's grid was designed in the 19th century, it's the only diagonal street on the island. It's confused many a tourist. Fortunately, New Yorkers are quick to show you the way.

❺ CHARGING BULL

Broadway at Bowling Green

www.chargingbull.com

The bull was a response to the stock market crash in the 1980s. Arturo Di Modica dropped the sculpture in front of the New York Stock Exchange as a Christmas present to New York. Now it's a favorite selfie spot for tourists, although usually not from the front of the sculpture.

❻ CAFE GRUMPY

20 Stone St.

www.cafegrumpy.com

+1 646-838-9306

🕐 Mo.-Fr. 6 a.m.-8 p.m., Sa.-Su. 8 a.m.-4 p.m.

Many coffee connoisseurs consider this to be the best coffee in New York. It's also very cozy. One thing's for sure: you won't leave in a bad mood.

❼ STONE STREET

In the past nobody wanted ships to sail to America empty, so they were filled with cobblestones. These were traded in downtown Manhattan for beaver hides and other goods.

The European cobblestones were used to pave Stone Street. This is now one of the only streets where you can sit and drink alcohol outside. So it's not only the beer that comes from the Netherlands, but also the cobblestones.

❽ NEW YORK STOCK EXCHANGE

11 Wall St.

www.nyse.com

+1 212-656-3000

🕐 Mo.-Fr. 9:30 a.m.-4 p.m.

You can only go inside the New York Stock Exchange if you're part of a publicly-traded company. So maybe this is the ideal moment to make your American dream come true and start your own company. Who knows? Before you know it, you may be the one ringing the bell to announce the beginning or the end of the trading day.

❾ FEARLESS GIRL

11 Wall Street

Fearless Girl is a work of art created by the artist Kristen Visbal, and was placed in front of the *Charging Bull* to celebrate International Women's Day in 2017. Its great success led to dangerous traffic situations. This was solved by relocating her to the New York Stock Exchange, where the Bull had originally stood before it was moved to another location.

⑩ TRINITY CHURCH

75 Broadway

www.trinitywallstreet.org

+1 212-602-0800

This church holds a special place in my heart because it's where the funeral was held for my good friend Joyce (See *BE NY From Tourist to New Yorker*). Trinity Church is a very affluent church since it was granted much land by Queen Anne of England. Now the Church board leases some of its property for exorbitant fees. So the church is just another Financial District player.

⑪ WALL STREET

When you hear 'Wall Street' you think men in suits and money. It used to be different. After Peter Minuit bought the island from the Native Americans, the Dutch built a wall around it to keep them and other colonists out. The street next to the wall was thus called Wall Street.

⑫ FEDERAL HALL

26 Wall St.

www.nps.gov

+1 212-825-6990

🕐 Mo.-Fr. 9 a.m.-5 p.m.

Federal Hall is where George Washington was sworn in as President. This explains the enormous statue of him in front of the building. A client once asked me if the statue is life-sized... What do you think?

⑬ FEDERAL RESERVE BANK OF NEW YORK

33 Liberty St.

www.newyorkfed.org

+1 212-720-6130

🕐 Mo.-Fr. 11:15 a.m.-3 p.m.

There is more gold in this bank than any other single place in the world. You can visit the building if you make reservations ahead of time. It's worth seeing how the safes are fastened to the ground. The ground is one of the hardest types of stone on the planet and is also what makes it possible for Manhattan to support so many skyscrapers. So the safes are really safe.

FUN FACT

There's a man in New York who looks for gold in the cracks on the sidewalks. He can make up to $600 a week doing this.

⑭ PEARL STREET PLAYGROUND

49 Fulton St.

www.nycgovparks.org

+1 212-639-9675

Oysters were so popular in New York City in the 19th century that they used all the shells to pave Pearl Street, which is how it got its name. You won't find any oysters in the playground but there is sand, water, and play facilities in this beautiful open space. Ideal for a short break.

⑮ IPIC THEATERS

11 Fulton St.

www.ipictheaters.com

+1 212-776-8272

🕐 Mo.-Su. 10:30 a.m.-11:30 p.m.

Movie-going in style. Want to sink into a leather sofa with a blanket and extra pillows, while the waiter serves you food prepared by a chef? It sounds too good to be true, but it's all possible in New York. Don't forget to make reservations.

⑯ SOUTH STREET SEAPORT MUSEUM

12 Fulton St.

www.southstreetseaportmuseum.org

+1 212-848-8600

🕐 We.-Su. 11 a.m.-5 p.m.

South Street Seaport is moving up as a neighborhood. This museum tells the story of New York's growth as a port and its role in the development of the United States. Via historic buildings, ancient ships, and interactive exhibitions, children can learn new things without even realizing they're learning.

⑰ IMAGINATION PLAYGROUND

Front St.

www.nycgovparks.org

+1 212-639-9675

🕐 Mo.-Su. 9 a.m.-5 p.m.

A playground specially designed to allow children to use their imagination. They can stack enormous blocks, build sand castles, or experiment with tubes and other instruments in running water. Approved by Marie!

FUN FACT

It's illegal to throw a ball at someone's head for your own amusement.

---

⑱ PIER 15

www.nycedc.com

🕐 Mo.-Su. 6 a.m.-midnight

This waterfront used to be completely neglected. Now, it's a fine location for repose among greenery, benches, and a magnificent view of the East River and the city.

⑲ NY WATERWAY

www.nywaterway.com

You have two options here: You could either take the boat to Governors Island (only in the summer) or to Brooklyn. You need to buy a ferry ticket ($2.75) in advance or by using the NYC Ferry app. Go on deck for the best view.

PART 2: VINTAGE COWBOY BOOTS

① FERRY BROOKLYN BRIDGE PARK / ATLANTIC AVENUE STOP

A convenient ferry stop that takes you to part 2 of the walk through the newly constructed Brooklyn Bridge Park. Disembark straight into a paradise playground.

② WATER LAB & SLIDE PARADISE & SWING VALLEY

Brooklyn Bridge Park Greenway

www.brooklynbridgepark.org

This playground has a water lab, a mountain you can slide on, a sand village, and ropes to swing from like Tarzan and Jane. Time to really let yourself go.

③ BROOKLYN BRIDGE PARK - PIER 6 - BEACH VOLLEYBALL COURTS

Brooklyn Bridge Park Greenway

www.brooklynbridgepark.org

+1 347-938-1394

🕐 Mo.-Sa. 6 a.m.-1 a.m.,

Sa. 6 a.m.-midnight

Are your kids too old for the swings? Look for the beach volleyball courts up ahead. There's a real community atmosphere here. If you didn't bring your own ball, you can always join the New York teenagers from the 'hood' for a game.

④ PICNIC PENINSULA PLAYGROUND

The perfect place for a barbecue, where the children can live it up in the playground while you're cooking. Before you head to the nearest supermarket to stock up on dogs and drumsticks, you may want to know that you usually have to share a grill: there are only 22, shared by 2.6 million Brooklynites and even more tourists.

⑤ JORALEMON STREET

It's quid pro quo! If you manage to climb this steep street you can reward yourself with an ice cream (see #6).

6 HÄAGEN-DAZS ICE CREAM SHOP

120 Montague St.
www.haagendazs.us
+1 718-979-3700
Mo.-Su. noon-9 p.m.

Häagen-Dazs was invented in New York in 1961. In his Bronx apartment, Reuben Mattis, Häagen-Dazs' creator, came up with a name he thought sounded Danish. He associated Denmark with creamy dairy products and valued the country's fair treatment of the Jews in WWII. His thought-up name was somewhat flawed however, since neither the ä nor the letter combination zs exists in Danish. Fortunately, that had no effect on the success of his ice cream.

7 BROOKLYN HEIGHTS PROMENADE

The splendid Brooklyn Heights Promenade is a great place for a stroll. The benches with the view of the Manhattan skyline make you feel like you're in a movie. That's probably because you've already seen this promenade on TV or at the cinema.

8 70 WILLOW STREET

Dan Houser, creator of the *Grand Theft Auto* videogame, bought this stately home in 2012 for 12.5 million dollars. Back then it was the most expensive house in the neighborhood. Nowadays, you can't get anything in that area for that kind of money. It's one of the most expensive neighborhoods in New York.

9 PEDESTRIAN BRIDGE TO PROMENADE

Squibb Park Bridge
The best way to reach the waterfront again is via this beautiful suspension bridge.

10 I HOTEL BROOKLYN BRIDGE

60 Furman St.
www.1hotels.com
+1 877-803-1111

This magnificent hotel is the 'talk of the town.' Everything is based on sustainability. It was constructed almost entirely out of recycled materials and many rooms have a spectacular view. That is also true of to the swimming pool on the roof. If you're staying here, don't hesitate to invite me. It's been my dream to swim a couple of laps up there one day.

11 BROOKLYN ICE CREAM FACTORY

1 Water St.
www.brooklynicecreamfactory.com
+1 718-246-3963
Mo.-Su. noon-10 p.m.

Where better to eat an ice cream than in the factory where it's made? And using the best ingredients. Visiting the Brooklyn Ice Cream Factory is a tradition for many New York families, and tourists are wisely making it theirs, too.

12 THE RIVER CAFÉ

1 Water St.
www.rivercafe.com
+1 718-522-5200
Mo.-Fr. 8:30 a.m.-11:30 a.m. and 5:30 p.m.-11 p.m.

The restaurant is on a boat under Brooklyn Bridge. Few restaurants have such a breathtaking view of downtown Manhattan, but their menu is also worth seeing. The River Café is also justifiably known as one of the most romantic restaurants in New York City.

13 JULIANA'S

19 Old Fulton St.
www.julianaspizza.com
+1 718-596-6700
Mo.-Su. 11:30 a.m.-3:15 p.m. and 4 p.m.-10 p.m.

Competition between Juliana's and Grimaldi's

has raged for years. Which of the two makes the best pizza? Even my city guide friends can't agree.

⑭ GRIMALDI'S

1 Front St.
www.grimaldis-pizza.com
+1 718-858-4300
🕐 Mo.-Fr. 11:30 a.m.-10:45 p.m., Sa. noon-11:45 p.m., Su. noon-10:45 p.m.
If you want to know the answer you'll just have to try them both. I myself have never conducted this ultimate test. After having our wedding pictures taken on the waterfront, we simply went to Grimaldi's.

⑮ ST. ANN'S WAREHOUSE

45 Water St.
www.stannswarehouse.org
+1 718-254-8779
This former warehouse is now a charming theater. Besides concerts and plays, it also presents puppet shows, for which it has a special affinity. Every spring the theater is home to Labapalooza!, a festival strictly dedicated to puppet theater.

⑯ JANE'S CAROUSEL

Old Dock St., on the waterfront
🕐 Th.-Su. 11 a.m.-6 p.m.
For both adults and children, no visit to Dumbo is complete without a ride on Jane's Carousel. This classic horses merry-go-round is encased in glass so you can enjoy the 'ride with head-spinning views', as the New York Times described it, all year long.

⑰ BROOKLYN HISTORICAL SOCIETY

55 Water St.
www.brooklynhistory.org
+1 718-222-4111
Want to know how many times Dumbo (Down Under the Manhattan Bridge Overpass) has had to reinvent itself? Almost as often as Lady Gaga. Well... that may be taking it too far. But whatever happens, Dumbo is here to stay. The neighborhood has never been more popular. There are even t-shirts for sale with the slogan, 'I live in Manhattan because I can't afford Brooklyn.'

⑱ FEED SHOP & CAFE

55 Water St.
www.feedprojects.com
929-397-2716
🕐 Mo.-Sa. 8 a.m.-7 p.m., Su. 8 a.m.-6 p.m.
Lauren Pierce Bush, George H. W. Bush's granddaughter, established FEED in order to end world hunger. When you buy a shopping bag or purse, the proceeds go to fund school meals for children in developing countries. The school lunch is often their only meal. Every bag has a number on it representing the number of meals you sponsor by buying it. Take the stairs (or the elevator) to the top floor of the Empire Store for a magnificent rooftop bar with a view of the Brooklyn Bridge.

⑲ CECCONI'S

55 Water St.
www.cecconisdumbo.com
+1 718-650-3900
🕐 Mo.-Sa. 11:30 a.m.-midnight, Su. 11:30 a.m.-11:30 p.m.
Feel like eating outside? Apart from the rooftops, there aren't many places in New York where that's possible. But it is at this classic Italian restaurant. Enjoy a glass of wine or the handmade pasta while you admire the skyline.

⑳ PEBBLE BEACH

Manhattan Bridge Pedestrian Path
www.brooklynbridgepark.org
You can dip your toes in the East River, here. If for no other reason than to be able to say you did.

21 PERFECT PICTURE – EMPIRE STATE BUILDING UNDER THE MANHATTAN BRIDGE

Washington St. and Water St.

No one can resist taking a picture of the Empire State Building fitting precisely under the Manhattan Bridge.

A tip from the pros: Only photographers with serious skills can take a photo from Washington Street and Front Street. Here's where you can discover whether it's time to start thinking about a new career.

22 GLEASON'S GYM

130 Water St.

www.gleasonsgym.com

+1 718-797-2872

🕐 Mo.-Fr. 5 a.m.-10 p.m.,
Sa.-Su. 8 a.m.-6 p.m.

This gym is the oldest, continuously operating boxing gym in the United States, and is also known as 'the cathedral of boxing.' It has produced 134 world champions, two Olympic gold medalists, and hundreds of amateur champs. Take a look at the ring where Muhammad Ali used to train, or hop into the gift shop. It doesn't get more authentic than this.

23 BROOKLYN ROASTING COMPANY

25 Jay St.

www.brooklynroasting.com

+1 718-855-1000

🕐 Mo.-Su. 7 a.m.-7 p.m.

You'll have a hard time refusing a cup of coffee at the Brooklyn Roasting Company. The aroma penetrating your nose as soon as you set foot inside is absolutely irresistible. Sometimes I think the smell alone gives me all the caffeine I need. Why not buy a bag of coffee for home? Extra perk: your whole house will be filled with that delicious aroma.

24 SUBWAY F TRAIN

With the F train you're in Midtown Manhattan in no time. Maybe why Dumbo is such a popular place to live.

LANGUAGES: ENGLISH, HEBREW AND SPANISH

FAVORITE SNACK: SEAWEED

SECRET PLACE: BROOKLYN BOWL

HOBBIES: CLIMBING, GYM, SCOUTS

FAVORITE FOOD: POKÉ

MUSEUM: MUSEUM OF MATHEMATICS

FAVORITE PLAYGROUND: ALL THE PLAYGROUNDS IN CENTRAL PARK

FAVORITE DAY OF THE YEAR: HALLOWEEN

SHIRA CLIMB TO THE TOP

If you think all American kids only like to eat hamburgers, think again. Our friend Shira prefers poké and adores seaweed. Maybe this gives her superpowers because, although she's still very young, she's a true sportswoman. Excelling at sports is one way of getting into a prestigious university. It helps you avoid having to take out a mega loan; who can say no to that? Shelling out $65,000 a year on tuition ain't easy. So let's hope Marie will become an athlete too.

When I discovered I had a fear of heights, I started to climb walls. It was my way of overcoming my fears. Another fear I had to conquer was the fear of public speaking. So I became a city guide.
One person who has always felt comfortable at high altitude is Shira (9). Climbing has become her biggest hobby. She trains for more than 5 hours a week to literally get to the top. Every Saturday she competes with her friends, climbing like a monkey, to reach the summit first. As a young girl with two older brothers, she can certainly hold her own.

Shira isn't unique simply because she won't go to dance classes like all the other girls. She's also different in her culinary tastes. She doesn't care much for burgers and shakes. No, her favorite food is poké, the traditional Hawaiian dish with fresh fish and vegetables. Needless to say, she was overjoyed when her uncle, Shay, my best New York friend, opened his new restaurant, Hokey Poké. When she can, Shira calls her Uncle Shay and asks him to prepare a bowl of poké for her. She knows exactly what has to go in it. Some brown rice and *courgetti* (spaghetti-shaped zucchini), cuts of fresh salmon, corn, radish, edamame beans (green soybeans), sunflower seeds, avocado, crunchy onions, spicy ginger vinaigrette, and wakame seaweed. Not seaweed salad, not nori, but wakame seaweed. Instead of the different types of Big Mac, New York children know the different types of seaweed. Eat that, McDonald's!

⊜ SOME TIPS FROM SHIRA

BROOKLYN BOULDERS
575 Degraw St., Dumbo, Brooklyn
23-10 41st Ave., Long Island City, Queens
www.brooklynboulders.com
+1 347-834-9066
Mo.-Fr. 7 a.m.-midnight, Sa.-Su. 8 a.m.-10 p.m.
Suppose you want to climb the Empire
State Building effortlessly, just like
King Kong? Go practice at Brooklyn
Boulders. If you're in the Queens
branch, after the session you could go
for ribs at John Brown Smokehouse,
the locals' absolute favorite.

FÜN FACT
Rendering the CGI model of the Empire
State Building for the movie King
Kong (2005) took 18 months. Just for
comparison's sake: the real building took
14 months to build.

BROOKLYN BOWL
61 Wythe Ave., Williamsburg, Brooklyn
www.brooklynbowl.com
+1 718 963 3369
Sa. 11 a.m.-5 p.m., Su. 11 a.m.-6 p.m.
There's a magnificent bowling alley hidden
away in trendy Williamsburg. Bowling among
the Williamsburg hipsters? Check. Do as the
locals do.

NATIONAL MUSEUM OF MATHEMATICS
11 E 26th St., between Madison Ave. and 5th Ave., NoMad
www.momath.org
+1 212-542-0566
Mo.-Su. 10 a.m.-5 p.m.
Whether you like math or not, you certainly
won't be bored in this museum. You'd be amazed
how interesting mathematics can be. This is one
of the only museums open every day of the year,
except on Thanksgiving Day. However, doors
close at 2:30 p.m. on the first Wednesday of every
month. Good for children 6 and older.

⊜ A TIP FROM PATRICK

HOKEY POKÉ
805 3rd Ave., in Crystal Pavilion, Midtown
www.hokeypokenyc.com
+1 212-754-3012
Mo.-Fr. 11 a.m.-4 p.m.
An instantly addictive Hawaiian specialty. The
poké joints are popping up like mushrooms, but
Hokey Poké is still the best.

CATCH THE BALL

Baseball, basketball, football, hockey, soccer. And don't forget the US Open, the New York City Marathon, and the Amateur Boxing Golden Gloves in Madison Square Garden. Is that enough to convince you that New York is one of the most important sports cities in the world? Want to see the best athletes in action? This is your big chance!

BASEBALL
THE NEW YORK METS VS. THE NEW YORK YANKEES

The Yankees are the more chic club, with fans from Manhattan and the suburbs. A ticket can cost up to $500 but you get the chance to eat Shake Shack burgers during the game. The Yankees' colors are blue and white. You might even be wearing the home colors without realizing it...

The Mets are the underdogs who hardly ever win. Their fans come from Queens and Brooklyn and pay $15 for a ticket. It's almost like they're being bribed to come to the game. The Mets' unique colors, blue and orange, are a combination you won't find in many closets. Except maybe in Dutch ones.

TENNIS

Want to see Serena Williams or Roger Federer up close? The US Open starts in August in Queens. All you need to get to this Grand Slam tournament is the 7 train. And a huge wallet.
www.usopen.org

THE NEW YORK CITY MARATHON

The largest marathon in the world, and with good reason. More than 50,000 participants cheered on by more than a million spectators. The whole of New York is enthralled by the event and, in every borough, hordes of spectators spend hours encouraging the runners. The only moments during the marathon when the cheering stops is when the runners cross the bridges, since spectators aren't allowed on them. Anybody who has participated will tell you what a unique experience it is to run the marathon here. So if you're the running type, go for it!
www.tcsnycmarathon.org

All the runners who discard clothing on the way actually donate it to charity. After the marathon, all the clothes are gathered and given to an organization for the homeless. The booty? Somewhere between 40,000 and 80,000 (!) lbs. of clothing.

FᴜN FACT

The first New York City Marathon was held in 1970 with 127 participants who ran four laps around Central Park.

MADISON SQUARE GARDEN
4 Pennsylvania Plaza, 8th Ave. and W 31st St., Midtown
www.msg.com

Only in a metropolis like New York would they build an arena in the middle of the city. Madison Square Garden is home to the Knicks and the Rangers. And every now and then, the living room is rented out to the likes of Bon Jovi, the Red Hot Chili Peppers, Adele, Justin Bieber, and even the occasional fellow countryman of mine.

FᴜN FACT

The changing rooms at Madison Square Garden are round so the players can look each other in the eye. Good for teambuilding.

STARRING ON BROADWAY

There are three places in the world where it's worth going to a Broadway show: London, Las Vegas, and New York. If you can fill theaters of more than 5000 seats every night, the quality must be very high. Producers have a big enough budget for the best actors, breathtaking scenery, and the most beautiful costumes.

ON AND OFF BROADWAY

The difference between on and Off-Broadway has nothing to do with the location of the theater. Broadway is a street running all the way from downtown Manhattan to the Upper West Side. Most of the theaters are around Times Square.

Only theaters with more than 499 seats can call themselves Broadway theaters. Their productions and actors can also be nominated for the Tony Awards. Theaters with 100-499 seats are called Off-Broadway. Fewer than 100 seats is Off-Off-Broadway.

FUN FACT

'There's no I in Broadway.' Not only in the spelling, but also in the rows. Too many people were disappointed after thinking they had seats in row 1, when it was actually row I. So now, there are no more I rows.

☰ A TIP FROM PATRICK

TKTS TIMES SQUARE
7th Ave. and W 47th St., Times Square
www.tdf.org
+1 212-912-9770
Mo.-Sa. 10 a.m.-8 p.m., Su. 11 a.m.-8 p.m.
If you haven't booked tickets in advance, take your chances at TKTS, where last-minute tickets are sold for the same day. There's a chance you'll be sitting behind a pillar but it's probably worth it for the 20%, 30% and sometimes even 40% discount.

FROZEN (6 TO 101 YEARS)
St. James Theatre, 246 W 44th St., between 7th and 8th Aves., Times Square
www.jujamcyn.com
So your kid has tantrums during your trip. You can let loose here and join in with Elsa on 'Let it Goooooo.'

THE LION KING (6 TO 101 YEARS)
Minkoff Theater, 200 W 45th St. and Broadway, Times Square
www.lionking.com/tickets
This musical has been playing since 1997 and is number 5 on the list of longest-playing Broadway shows. And with good reason. The costumes are magnificent and the music from the Disney Movie is still breathtaking. Hakuna Matata!

THE BOOK OF MORMON (14 TO 101 YEARS)
Eugene O'Neil Theater, 230 W 49th St. between Broadway and 8th Ave., Times Square
www.jujamcyn.com
The perfect musical for South Park fans. The show is about Mormons contemplating religion while in the African jungle, told with a touch of humor. Although the show has no minimum age recommendation, this type of humor and explicit language may not be to everyone's taste. Tickets are on the expensive side and you need to book well ahead to make sure you get seats.

FUN FACT
It takes the actors in the Broadway musical The Lion King six weeks to learn to walk like giraffes.

YOU C[A]
NOT L[A]
PEOPL[E]
ANYM[O]

N

BEL

E

RE

ADELINE

LANGUAGES: <u>FRENCH AND ENGLISH</u>
WANTS TO BE: <u>PRESIDENT OR OLYMPIC SWIMMING CHAMPION</u>
HOBBIES: <u>SWIMMING, YOGA, PLAYING WITH BELLA THE PUPPY</u>
FAVORITE DAY: <u>CHRISTMAS</u>
MUSEUM: <u>EXHIBITIONS ON FASHION IN THE MET AND MOMA</u>
FAVORITE SNACK: <u>FRUIT, PROTEIN BARS</u>

MANON SINK OR SWIM

When I was the manager of a restaurant, my previous job here in New York, I liked entertaining the children so their parents could eat in peace. Sometimes I think that even back then, without realizing it, I was preparing myself for my job as a city guide, which is also a form of entertainment, *and* for my role as a father, two things that make me really happy. I got to know some great kids at the restaurant, who kept coming back every week. For instance, Manon (10) and her brother Olivier, an athletic girl and an energetic boy, who were always glad to see me again. The feeling was mutual, of course. Now, so many years later, I imagine Marie becoming just as athletic and ambitious as Manon.

Many people could learn from Manon's perseverance, her focus, and her passion for her sport. She enjoys training four times a week for an hour and a half. On top of that, on weekends she participates in tournaments in New York or in other states, which means she's often away from home. In her spare time she likes playing with her puppy, Bella, doing yoga with her mother, or watching tennis. Every year she watches the US Open, the last of the four Grand Slam tournaments, from the stands. Fans from all over the world try to find tickets to see their idols playing in Queens.

Nancy, Manon and Olivier's mother, used to work for GAP and later for Ralph Lauren. She created a platform for the staff, where colleagues could share things on an internal network. She called it the virtual Times Square. It was a meeting place where people could share tips, recipes, trivia, and pics. Manon and Olivier have undoubtedly been brought up to be open to different cultures and ideas. It's evident that their inherent curiosity is being stimulated. Manon reads many books, likes to try food from different countries, and loves visiting museums, especially if there's a fashion exhibition. That's why the Met and the MoMA are her favorites. Manon even once participated in a fashion show. Don't think her mother has anything to say about which clothes Manon will wear. Little girls grow up.
Olivier is also very fashion-conscious. He's only eight years old but already has quite a collection of ties in his closet. He can stand for a long time in front of his closet trying to choose the right tie for a special occasion. He's right. Clothes make the man. In New York for sure.

⊜ A FEW TIPS FROM MANON

LASKER POOL
110th St. and Lenox Ave., Central Park
www.nycgovparks.org
+1 212-534-7639
Mo.-Su. 11 a.m.-3 p.m. and 4 p.m.-7 p.m.
This Olympic swimming pool is a
must for every swimming freak.
Do you really want to swim laps?
Do as Manon does, and take a dip
between 7 and 8:30 a.m. or between
7 p.m. and sunset, alongside swimming champs from Harlem and the
Upper West Side.

METROPOLITAN MUSEUM OF ART (THE MET)
1000 5th Ave. and E 82nd St., Upper East Side
www.metmuseum.org
+1 212-731-1498
Su.-Th. 10 a.m.-5:30 p.m., Fr.-Sa. 10 a.m.-9 p.m.
The largest art museum in the United
States has more than 2 million works
of art. Special maps and guides are
available for children and are free
from the information desk. Special
workshops are also offered for families. You can find information about
them on the website. Children under 12 get in for free.

FUN FACT

Every week a Dutch florist, Remco van Vliet,
makes bouquets for the Metropolitan
Museum of Art. Some bouquets are more
than 20 feet tall.

SWIMMING POOLS

Nothing works better than a cool dip if you want to escape the summer heat. This is why the outdoor swimming pools in New York are free for everyone. They're open from the end of June until Labor Day (the first Monday in September), between 11 a.m. and 7 p.m. (Note: they're closed between 3 and 4 p.m. for cleaning.)

DO'S AND DON'TS

Wearing a swimsuit is compulsory. If it's really hot, you're allowed to wear a white t-shirt over your suit to protect you from sunburn. This rule was created to ward off gang members, who always wear their gang t-shirts.

Armbands and the like are discouraged because they can provide a false sense of security. Children who don't know how to swim have to stay in the shallow end. Bring a stroller at your own risk; there isn't always a safe place to leave it. Bring a strong lock too, so you can safely store your valuables in a locker.

NICE OUTDOOR POOLS

CARMINE STREET SWIMMING POOL
1 Clarkson St. and 7th Ave., Greenwich Village
www.nycgovparks.org
+1 212-242-5418
Mo.-Su. 11 a.m.-3 p.m. and 4 p.m.-7 p.m.
Swimming with a view of Keith Haring murals? A good way to impress your friends.

TOMPKINS SQUARE POOL
Ave. A between E 7th and E 10th St., East Village
www.nycgovparks.org
+1 212-639-9675
Mo.-Su. 11 a.m.-3 p.m. and 4 p.m.-7 p.m.
A miniature swimming pool that's perfect for small children because it's only 36 inches deep. Other reasons to go to Tompkins Square Park include a basketball court, ping-pong tables, and a playground.

NICE INDOOR POOL

SPORTSPARK
250 Main Street, Roosevelt Island
+1 212-832-4514
For only $7 for adults and $3 for children, you can jump off the diving board to your heart's content.

COOL DOWN IN THE SPRINKLERS

If you want to cool off in the fountains you should bring water shoes. In some cases swimsuits, swim diapers, a towel, and spare clothes could be useful.

FIRE HYDRANTS

Nothing epitomizes New York summers more than a fireman spraying squealing children. Although it's illegal to open a fire hydrant by yourself, you can always ask a fireman to do it. The wet fun can go on until it gets dark.

DON'T SKIP THESE (WATER) PLAYGROUNDS

There's an abundance of playgrounds in New York and some of them are really worth a detour. Your children are guaranteed a good time there.

ANCIENT PLAYGROUND IN CENTRAL PARK
85th St and 5th Ave., Upper East Side
www.centralparknyc.org
Mo.-Su. 6 a.m.-1 a.m.
The Ancient Playground is situated not far from the Metropolitan Museum of Art. This playground is, in fact, not at all ancient but inspired by the Met's Egyptian Art Department. Since the playground was recently renovated for almost three million dollars, everything still looks brand new. Ideal after a visit to the museum.

IMAGINATION PLAYGROUND
Front St. and John St., South Street Seaport
www.centralparknyc.org
+1 212-639-9675
Mo.-Su. 9 a.m.-5 p.m.
The playground was designed by the architect David Rockwell. He thought that most playgrounds look the same and don't adequately allow children to use their imagination. But at the Imagination Playground children can build with blocks, build sand castles, or experiment with tubes and other implements in running water. (Note: there isn't much shade.)

TEARDROP PARK
Warren St. and Murray St., Battery Park City
www.bpcparks.org
This hidden playground has a large slide, fun sprinklers, and rocks to clamber on. There's lots of shade and you're completely surrounded by greenery. Here, the chaotic, hectic metropolis seems miles away.

SHOP TILL YOU DROP

If it's too hot or even too cold, you could always go shopping in the large, elegant, air-conditioned stores. You could spend a whole week in department stores such as Bloomingdale's, Macy's, Barney's, Saks Fifth Avenue, and Lord & Tailor. Then there are also the magnificent flagship stores on Fifth Avenue and the high-end luxury stores on Madison Avenue, the unique shops in SoHo, the original shops on the Lower East Side, and the beautiful Westfield and Brookfield Place in downtown Manhattan.

MACY'S HERALD SQUARE
151 W 34th St., between Broadway and 7th Ave.
www.macys.com
Mo.-Sa. 10 a.m.-10 p.m., Su. 10 a.m.-9 p.m.
Use these pro tips to get the best out of your shopping trip to Macy's:
- The stores are uncrowded on weekdays before lunchtime.
- In the winter it's convenient to leave your coat in the cloakroom.
- Clients from outside the U.S. can get a 10% discount card at the Visitors' Center.
- American customers can have their purchases home-delivered.
- Take a well-earned break in one of the many food and beverage establishments. The Starbucks in the beautiful Herald Square Café is an ideal place for coffee, champagne, and hot chocolate.

GAP
1514 Broadway, Times Square
And other locations in Manhattan
www.gap.com
+1 646-688-5850
Mo.-Su. 8 a.m.-2 a.m.
Didn't bring enough clothes for the offspring? Everything dirty after a day of gamboling in the Central Park playgrounds? You'll find fashionable basics at GAP.

⊜ A TIP FROM INEKE

JANIE AND JACK
1150 3rd Ave. and E 67th St., Upper East Side
www.janieandjack.com
+1 212-988-4120
Mo.-Sa. 10 a.m.-7 p.m., Su. 11 a.m.-6 p.m.
Shop like the Upper East Side fancy kids at Janie and Jack for an outfit to wear for a high tea. Their dresses and suits are guaranteed to turn heads when you make an entrance at the Palm Court in the Plaza Hotel. I bought Marie's first outfit here. She only got to wear it for two weeks before growing out of it. But it was more than worth it for the cute photos.

FAVORITE DAY OF THE YEAR: <u>WESTMINSTER DOG SHOW IN MADISON SQUARE GARDEN</u>

LIKES: <u>TAKING WALKS IN CENTRAL PARK</u>

SPEAKS: <u>LABRADORIAN</u>

UNDERSTANDS: <u>ENGLISH</u>

FAVORITE STORE: <u>WAG WEAR</u>

FAVORITE SNACK: <u>PRETZEL SHAPED DOG SNACKS BY BARK</u>

FAVORITE PLACE IN NEW YORK: <u>CARL SCHURZ PARK</u>

LIVES IN: <u>UPPER EAST SIDE, MANHATTAN</u>

FRASIER DON'T FORGET THE DOG

In New York more money is spent on children than on anything else. Or maybe not. Dogs can probably claim first place. Fortunately, Ineke and I agree on one thing: both of us love animals but prefer not having any at home. Our hands are already full with our little Marie and money just slips through our fingers. The day care center easily costs $2000 a month. It's money well spent but means a dog is not an option. But, happily, we can always borrow Tom's and Matthew's dog. They gladly let Marie cuddle their black Labrador, Frasier, or take her for walks in Central Park. Good for Marie, good for Frasier, and therefore good for us.

Frasier is a genuine New York jetsetter. As you may have read in my first book, *BE NY From Tourist to New Yorker*, she divides her time, along with Tom and Matthew, between the Upper East Side, the Hamptons, and Miami. When her owners are working she stays at the doggy daycare, although she does have her own dog walker who takes her out every day. If you walk down the street in New York, the dog walkers are easily identifiable from afar: they usually take out five or more dogs at once. Be careful not to get tangled up in all those leashes. As with your baby, you wouldn't entrust your best four-legged friend to just anyone. A professional dog walker must have good references. It pays well; you can earn $15 an hour. Per dog, that is. So that big bunch of dogs isn't such a bad idea.

If your pet is suffering from burnout from its demanding dog's life, it can always go to a dog psychiatrist, a massage parlor, or a dog spa. When it's birthday time, you throw a party for all its furry friends and their owners. Seriously; in New York this is no joke. Nice presents are, for example, Petboxes or Pawpacks, a monthly surprise box full of all kinds of toys. One of the biggest events is the Halloween Dog Parade in Tompkins Square Park. The week before Halloween, all the dogs gather to compete for the title of best-costumed dog. Over the top? No way? Any excuse for a party is good enough for a New Yorker.

One more tidbit: dogs aren't allowed into any venue serving food. But there's a solution. Just use one of Dog Parker's many doghouses. Using an app and the puppy-cam, you can see how your furry friend is doing. In the meantime, you can quickly get a bite to eat or even catch up on some shopping. On one of my recent tours a nice lady asked if she could install her husband in one...

A TIP FROM FRASIER

ASK THE DOG
Lost? Need a tip for a good restaurant? Ask anyone with a dog. There's a good chance they live in the neighborhood.

A TIP FROM MARIE

CAN I SAY HI?
Want to pet a dog you meet on the street? Ask its owner first. If allowed, let the dog sniff your hand first as a way of introducing yourself.

FUN FACT
During superstorm Sandy, downtown Manhattan suffered a power outage that lasted several days. In Midtown, hotel suites were rented in the Plaza Hotel for dogs that were staying at doggy daycares without electricity.

DOG PARKS

CARL SCHURZ PARK
E 86th St. and East End Ave., Upper East Side
Open 24 hours
With a view of the East River, Roosevelt Island and the Queensboro Bridge, this park is a fantastic location for walking your dog. While you're there you could go see Gracie Mansion. This is the official residence of the Mayor of the City of New York, currently occupied by Bill de Blasio and his family. After that, take a long walk along the East River.

WASHINGTON SQUARE PARK
Between Washington Square W and Washington Square E at the end of Fifth Ave.
www.nycgovparks.org
Open 24 hours
This park has separate small and large dog runs. It's also one of the only parks where dogs are allowed on the grass. The ideal place to sunbathe with your furry friend.

PASS

DOG FRIENDLY

LUCKYDOG: DOG-FRIENDLY BAR
303 Bedford Ave., between S 1st St. and S 2nd St., Williamsburg, Brooklyn
Mo.-Su. noon-4 a.m.
This bar has a patio where dogs can run around while their owners relax with a drink.

BORIS & HORTON
195 Avenue A and E 12th St., East Village
www.borisandhorton.com
Mo.-Su. 7 a.m.-11 p.m.
The first dog-friendly cafe, where you can sip coffee, tea, beer, or wine with your dog. Includes a shop where you can buy accessories, such as a special dog carrier bag.

FAKE SERVICE DOGS
Dog regulations are pretty vague. Dogs aren't allowed in most stores and restaurants unless they're trained 'service dogs.' But you don't need a permit. So many people buy fake labels on the internet so they can take their dogs with them everywhere. You may see movie stars dining in top restaurants with their dog in a designer handbag. They're most probably slipped an occasionally piece of meat to keep them quiet.

FUN FACT
In New York dogs are allowed on the subway only if they're carried in a bag.

LET'S GO DOG SHOPPING

DOG & CO
1000 8th Ave., underground in TurnStyle Market, Columbus Circle, Upper West Side
www.shopdogandco.com
+1 646-351-0905
Mo.-Fr. 9 a.m.-8 p.m., Sa. 10 a.m.-6 p.m., Su. noon-6 p.m.
Here you'll find the most fashionable outfits for your dog, such as fur coats and boots to withstand the cold New York winters. They also sell enough toys here to help your pet forget it had to stay home during your trip to New York.

WAG WEAR
48 E 11th St., between University Pl. and Broadway, Greenwich Village
www.wagwear.com
+1 212-673-7210
Mo.-Sa. 11 a.m.-7 p.m., Su. noon-6 p.m.
This store sells 'puppy chic'–dog outfits in the latest trends. Classic gear your pet can sport on South Beach Miami as well as on the street in TriBeCa.

One in seven New Yorkers has at least one dog under his or her roof.

The most popular dog names in New York are Bella, Coco, and Lola for females and Max, Charlie, and Rocky for males.

FAMOUS INSTAGRAM DOGGIES

Dogs are extremely popular on Instagram. Of course, they're much cuter than humans...

ZAMMY THE GIANT SHEEPADOODLE (@ZAMMYPUP)
This Sheepadoodle (a cross between an Old English sheepdog and an XL poodle) was voted most fluffy dog on Instagram. Its day job is cuddling children in hospitals.

LULU NASTY (@LULUNASTY)
Don't let the name mislead you. Lulu is an upper-class dog. She likes lazing around by the pool and gazing at the skyline.

OSCAR WITH THE GOOD HAIR (@OSCARWITHTHEGOODHAIR)
This Tibetan terrier has the most gorgeous hair and the nicest habits.

MOCHI THE MODEL DOG (@MOCHIANDTHECITY)
A model who enjoys fashion, wine, and New York City.

LITTLE DUDE (@WORLDOFLITTLEDUDE)
This sweet, quiet dog teaches children social and emotional skills. He regularly visits classrooms and is also available as a stuffed animal.

HOW MUCH DOES A DOG COST PER MONTH?

$ 200 FOOD

$ 600 DOGGY DAYCARE

$ 15/h DOG WALKER

$ 35 TOYS

$ 25 PEDICURE

$ 100 DOG CARE

$ 700 BIRTHDAY PARTY

$ 70 CLOTHES

$ 100 PSYCHIATRIST

FROM CHICKEN WINGS TO HIPSTER KINGS

(12-21 YEARS)

5

DRIVING AROUND

East River

DRIVING AROUND

12-21 YEARS · **+/- 5.5 MILES**

EAST VILLAGE – NOLITA –
LOWER EAST SIDE – WILLIAMSBURG

PART 1: CHICKEN WINGS

1. BLACK SEED
2. MOMOFUKU NOODLE BAR
3. BRODO
4. OBSCURA ANTIQUES & ODDITIES
5. BORIS & HORTON
6. TOMPKINS SQUARE PARK
7. PINK OLIVE
8. MR. THROWBACK
9. ENCHANTMENTS
10. PLEASE DON'T TELL
11. PHYSICAL GRAFFITEA
12. DAN & JOHN'S WINGS
13. SEARCH & DESTROY
14. MCSORLEY'S OLD ALE HOUSE
15. THE STANDARD, EAST VILLAGE
16. THE BOWERY HOTEL
17. KITH
18. SUPREME
19. NEW MUSEUM
20. PUBLIC
21. THE BOX
22. MORGENSTERN'S FINEST ICE CREAM
23. GEM
24. RUSS & DAUGHTERS
25. THE BACK ROOM

SEE NEXT PAGE → → →

DRIVING AROUND

12-21 YEARS   **+/- 5.5 MILES**

EAST VILLAGE – NOLITA – LOWER EAST SIDE – WILLIAMSBURG

PART 2: HIPSTER KINGS

1. PETER LUGER STEAK HOUSE
2. FREEHOLD
3. VICE MEDIA LLC
4. DOMINO PARK
5. DEVOCIÓN
6. PACKAGE FREE
7. SUPREME BROOKLYN
8. NITEHAWK CINEMA
9. BY CHLOE
10. APPLE WILLIAMSBURG
11. WHOLE FOODS MARKET
12. JULIETTE
13. CAPRICES BY SOPHIE
14. BULLETIN
15. CAFE MOGADOR
16. EGG SHOP
17. HEATONIST
18. ROUGH TRADE NYC
19. BROOKLYN BOWL
20. THE WILLIAM VALE

This expedition will make you a New Yorker among New Yorkers. You start at East Village, where there are many exciting places to discover. From a speakeasy to shops with magic potions or vintage basketball jerseys. NoLIta is the neighborhood with the coolest sneakers and skating gear. Via the Williamsburg Bridge, we arrive at the neighborhood, which in recent years has evolved from shabby alternative to hipster chic. You'll find the best coffee joints here, as well as an old bowling alley and a splendid rooftop bar. Whatever you do, don't skip Williamsburg.

PART 1: CHICKEN WINGS

❶ BLACK SEED

176 1st Ave.
www.blackseedbagels.com
+1 646-484-5718
🕐 Mo.-Tu. 7 a.m-4 p.m., We.-Su. 7 a.m.-6 p.m.

The bagels are hand-rolled, boiled in honey water, and baked in a wood-fired oven. If you want to go the full New York, order an 'everything bagel' with lox and dill cream cheese.

❷ MOMOFUKU NOODLE BAR

171 1st Ave.
www.noodlebar-ny.momofuku.com
+1 212-777-7773
🕐 Mo.-Fr. noon-4:30 p.m. and 5:30 p.m.-11 p.m., Sa. noon-4 p.m. and 5:30 p.m.-1 a.m., Su. noon-4 p.m. and 5:30 p.m.-11 p.m.

There are always long lines here because the noodles they serve are not just any old noodles. According to noodle connoisseurs, these are simply the best in New York. But they also have other interesting dishes on the menu, which changes daily (!).

❸ BRODO

200 1st Ave.
www.brodo.com
+1 646-602-1300
🕐 Mo.-Fr. 8 a.m.-8 p.m., Sa.-Su. 10 a.m.-8 p.m.

Not a coffee or a tea lover? Brodo capitalizes on this by serving bouillon. This joint isn't much more than a large window in a wall, but the bouillon will give you the strength to complete your walk at a brisk pace.

❹ OBSCURA ANTIQUES & ODDITIES

207 Ave. A
www.obscuraantiques.com
+1 212-505-9251
🕐 Mo.-Su. noon-8 p.m.

It may surprise you, but this isn't even the strangest shop on this walk. They have mounted animals, dice made of bone, and amazing magic tricks. You can browse here for hours.

❺ BORIS & HORTON

195 Ave. A
www.borisandhorton.com
🕐 Mo.-Su. 7 a.m.-11 p.m.

Boris & Horton allows you and your dog to order a drink and socialize with the New York hounds. It's the East Village dog lovers' favorite hangout. You won't come across many tourists here.

❻ THOMPSON SQUARE PARK

E 10th St.
www.nycgovparks.org
+1 718-813-8971
🕐 Mo.-Su. 6 a.m.-midnight

The park is best known for its Halloween Dog Parade, where dogs in costume, um... parade. The park is also worth visiting the rest of the year, thanks to the large playgrounds, the basketball courts, and the small swimming pool. Another feature is the memorial fountain to the fire on the Slocum, a ship that burned down on the East River in 1904. More than 1000 passengers, mostly women and children, died in the disaster which, prior to 9/11, was the deadliest in New York City history.

7 PINK OLIVE
439 E 9th St.
www.pinkolive.com
+1 212-780-0036
🕐 Mo.-Fr. noon-8 p.m.,
Sa. 11 a.m.-7 p.m., Su. 11 a.m.-6 p.m.
This cute little shop has everything you never needed but always wanted. A neat card with 'You are my everything bagel' on it, a big tote proclaiming 'You are loved,' and more useless stuff I sometimes dare to buy for my wife.

8 MR. THROWBACK
437 E 9th St.
www.mrthrowback.com
+1 917-261-7834
🕐 Th.-Tu. noon-8 p.m.
As the name suggests, Mr. Throwback takes you back in time. They have sports gear, video games, and other games and toys from the 90s. Baseball and basketball fans come here to get a jersey displaying their favorite player's number.

9 ENCHANTMENTS
424 E 9th St.
www.enchantmentsincnyc.com
+1 212-228-4394
🕐 We.-Mo. 1 p.m.-8:45 p.m.
Do you have a wish? You'll definitely find what you want in the candles. The magical symbols carved into them will make your wish come true within seven days of lighting the candle. Enchantments also has all the ingredients you need for making a magic potion. They even sell a love potion.

10 PLEASE DON'T TELL
113 St. Marks Pl.
www.pdtnyc.com
+1 212-614-0386
🕐 Su.-Th. 6 p.m.-2 a.m.,
Fr.-Sa. 6 p.m.-3 a.m.
When you enter this hot dog joint, you see an old phone booth. Remember those? One of those prehistoric boxes you go into to call someone. You have to dial a secret code when you enter and, with any luck, you'll be admitted to the clandestine cocktail bar that isn't so clandestine any more. But it's a great way to get in.

11 PHYSICAL GRAFFITEA
96 St. Marks Pl.
www.physicalgraffitea.com
+1 212-477-7334
🕐 Mo.-Su. 11 a.m.-10 p.m.
This is the place for delicious tea mélanges. Don't be intimidated by the several hundred jars with handwritten labels. Just ask for advice. Every ailment has a special tea to provide relief.

12 DAN & JOHN'S WINGS
135 1st Ave.
www.danandjohns.com
+1 917-456-8808
🕐 Mo.-Su. noon-midnight
If you want to taste the original Buffalo wings, you've got to go to Dan & John's, a.k.a. the Kings of Wings. During the Super Bowl, the whole of New York comes here for its wings. The name alone is reason enough to give it a shot.

⑬ SEARCH & DESTROY

25 St. Marks Pl. A

+1 212-358-1120

⏱ Mo.-Su. 1 p.m.-10 p.m.

The bloody carcass of a pig and a bondage mannequin make up the décor of this hardcore punk store. Not so suitable for the oversensitive. There's also a collection of vintage t-shirts. You'll definitely find the Halloween costume you've been looking for here.

⑭ MCSORLEY'S OLD ALE HOUSE

15 E 7th St.

www.mcsorleysoldalehouse.nyc

+1 212-473-9148

⏱ Mo.-Sa. 11 a.m.-1 a.m., Su. 1 p.m.-1 a.m.

The oldest saloon in New York, serving light and dark ales since 1854. Don't miss the handcuffs Houdini escaped from after being challenged by McSorley's owner. Previous guests include President Lincoln and John Lennon. Women have been admitted only since 1970. And the ladies' bathroom wasn't added until 1986.

⑮ THE STANDARD, EAST VILLAGE

25 Cooper Square

www.standardhotels.com

+1 212-475-5700

During the Christmas season, the hotel sets up a cozy wintery village with Christmas trees, small yurts with warm blankets, and Glühwein. A fine place for a cocktail or a meal the rest of the year too.

⑯ THE BOWERY HOTEL

335 Bowery

www.theboweryhotel.com

+1 212-505-9100

The Bowery Hotel's stylish lobby makes you think you're in London. The magnificent bar certainly won't disappoint. No relation to the Bowery Mission, further up the road, which offers shelter for the homeless.
A tip from Patrick: If you like podcasts and you want to know more about the history of New York, listen to *The Bowery Boys*.

⑰ KITH

337 Lafayette St.

www.kith.com

+1 646-648-6285

⏱ Mo.-Sa. 10 a.m.-9 p.m., Su. 11 a.m.-8 pm.

The best address for the hippest sneakers! As well as elegant sportswear for men, women, and children.

⑱ SUPREME

274 Lafayette St.

www.supremenewyork.com

⏱ Mo.-Sa. 11 a.m.-6 p.m., Su. noon-6 p.m.

Skateboarders, hip-hoppers, rockers, or anybody who feels young must visit to see their colorful collection. If the line is too long, just visit the other Supreme, which comes later on this walk.

⑲ NEW MUSEUM

235 Bowery

www.newmuseum.org

+1 212-219-1222

⏱ Tu.-Su. 11 a.m.-6 p.m., Th. 11 a.m.-9 p.m., Fr.-Su. 11 a.m.-6 p.m.

This museum is devoted solely to contemporary art. If you're not a lover of modern art, you can at least enjoy the amazing view. Admission is free for children aged 18 and under. On Thursday evenings between 7 and 9 p.m. admission is free for everyone.

⑳ PUBLIC

215 Chrystie St.

www.publichotels.com

In the mood to really live it up? Public Hotel is the downtown place to be. This is where to party with the rich and famous. It was originally intended as affordable luxury but, in New York, the term 'affordable' is open to interpretation.

㉑ THE BOX

189 Chrystie St.
www.theboxnyc.com
+1 212-982-9301
Tu.-Sa. 11 p.m.-4 a.m.

Suppose you have all the money in the world and have already seen it all? You crank it up a notch. The Box offers a mix of burlesque and nightlife and is one of the hardest clubs to get into. The shows are not suitable for the overly sensitive and are absolutely 21+. So, to be on the safe side, check the website before spending hours waiting in line. Golden tip: try to look as if you do this on a weekly basis. A confident attitude will improve your chances of making it past security.

㉒ MORGENSTERN'S FINEST ICE CREAM

2 Rivington St.
www.morgensternsnyc.com
+1 212-209-7684
Su.-Th. 8 a.m.-11 p.m., Fr.-Sa. 8 a.m.-midnight

Some of the ice cream here is black as coal. Not surprising, because that's what's in it. Three days later, your tongue is still black. Great for freaking out your friends. Apparently, this dark dessert isn't even bad for your health.

㉓ GEM

116 Forsyth St.
www.gem-nyc.com
Mo.-Su. 8 a.m.-5 p.m.

The youngest chef in Manhattan is 19 years old and this is his restaurant. Flynn McGarry named it after his mother, but then spelled her name backwards. The only option is the complete menu of 12 to 15 courses for $155. But Flynn cooks like a god. During the day, just have coffee and cake in The Living Room and enjoy the homey atmosphere.

㉔ RUSS & DAUGHTERS

127 Orchard St., between Delancey St. and Rivington St., NoLIta
www.shop.russanddaughters.com
+1 212-475-4880
Mo.-We. 8 a.m.-6 p.m., Th. 8 a.m.-7 p.m., Fr.-Su. 8 a.m.-6 p.m.

As a girl, Supreme Court justice Ruth Bader Ginsburg was already a Russ & Daughters fan. Most businesses are called '& Sons' but, thanks to Russ & Daughters, the future judge knew all her dreams would come true even before she'd ever heard the word feminism. All the more reason to try New York's best bagels.

㉕ THE BACK ROOM

102 Norfolk St.
www.backroomnyc.com
+1 212-228-5098
Su.-Th. 7:30 p.m.-3 a.m., Fr.-Sa. 7:30 p.m.-4 a.m.

Although Prohibition is a thing of the distant past, the speakeasies (a hidden bar where alcohol could be consumed when it was illegal) are still popular. The Back Room is one of the last authentic joints that have remained in existence since the twenties. Open the gate and go through the long alley until you reach a staircase. Go up the stairs and through the door. You can enjoy, as they did 85 years ago, a forbidden cocktail, served in disguised in a teacup.

FUN FACT

Between 1920 and 1933 the manufacturing and distribution of alcohol was outlawed in an attempt to banish alcoholism. Coctails were reinvented during Prohibition to mask the illegally distilled alcohol's bad flavor with other, tastier, ingredients.

FUN FACT

When the Williamsburg Bridge was opened in 1903, it was the world's last cable bridge.

PART 2: HIPSTER KINGS

① PETER LUGER STEAK HOUSE

178 Broadway
www.peterluger.com
+1 718-387-7400
🕐 Mo.-Th. 11:45 a.m.-9:45 p.m.,
Fr.-Sa. 11:45 a.m.-10:45 p.m.,
Su. 12:45 p.m.-9:45 p.m.

A steakhouse paradise for meat lovers that was even awarded a Michelin star. Reservations don't come easy, but you may get luckier with lunch. Cash only. Obviously, it's all about the dough here.

② FREEHOLD

43 S 3rd St.
www.freeholdbrooklyn.com
+1 718-388-7591
🕐 Mo.-Su. 7 a.m.-7 p.m.

Only in New York would you find a hotel without rooms. The 'reception' is actually a cloakroom, and the receptionist will give you Monopoly or Risk to play. You can work on your laptop in peace or play some ping-pong to loosen up your arms. On Sundays, there's free 'Sunrise Yoga' followed by a 'Lazy Brunch.'

③ VICE MEDIA LLC

49 S 2nd St.
www.vice.com
+1 718-599-3101

Vice has conquered the world with ground-breaking interviews and movies about art, culture, crime, fashion, and much more. This is one of their offices where the news is made. I can only dream of ever reaching their number of views.

④ DOMINO PARK

Grand St. and River St.
www.nycgovparks.org
+1 212-639-9675
Always open.

After seeing this brand new playground you'll know this neighborhood's future is guaranteed. Who knows, maybe your child will become friends here with the newest unicorn tech company's boss's hipster tyke. The Domino Sugar factory used to be located here and was also the inspiration for the playground. The idea is that a child goes in as a sugar beet and comes out again as a sugar cube. I hope it goes okay!

⑤ DEVOCIÓN

69 Grand St., between Kent Ave. and Barc Ave., Williamsburg, Brooklyn
www.devocion.com
+1 718-285-6180
🕐 Mo.-Fr. 7 a.m.-7 p.m.,
Sa.-Su. 8 a.m.-7 p.m.

All the bloggers come to work on their MacBooks in this magnificent coffee shop. But it is definitely an inspiring space, where brilliant ideas spontaneously pop into your head. Or is that the sound of percolating coffee in the background...?

⑥ PACKAGE FREE

137 Grand St.
www.packagefreeshop.com
🕐 Mo.-Su. 11 a.m.-7 p.m.

New York produces more garbage than any other city in the United States, but things are about to change. Stores that offer no packaging, such as this one, are popping up all over the place. So go ahead and take your own coffee cup when you're walking through the city. Besides helping the environment, you'll often get a 5 or 10 cent discount on your beverage. Saving money while saving the planet – it's possible!

7 SUPREME BROOKLYN

152 Grand St.

www.supremenewyork.com

+1 718-599-2700

Mo.-Sa. 11 a.m.-7 p.m., Su. noon-6 p.m.

The security guards are here to make sure no fights break out in the wait line. Don't despair when you see the line; it's all part of the true Supreme experience. You'll be rewarded by the chance to acquire a piece of clothing from the newest collection.

8 NITEHAWK CINEMA

136 Metropolitan Ave.

www.nitehawkcinema.com

+1 718-782-8370

The waiter takes your order before the show begins. Fried chicken sandwich or a kale salad while watching a movie? That's triple the fun.

9 BY CHLOE

171 N 3rd St.

www.eatbychloe.com

+1 347-379-4828

Mo.-Th. 11 a.m.-10 p.m., Fr. 11 a.m.-11 p.m., Sa. 10 a.m.-11 p.m., Su. 10 a.m.-10 p.m.

If you're still not convinced vegan food can be really tasty, you've got to go to By Chloe. Sweet potato air-baked fries with pesto meatballs? Wanna bet you won't miss that burger?

10 APPLE WILLIAMSBURG

247 Bedford Ave.

www.apple.com

+1 929-397-2740

Mo.-Fr. 10 a.m.-9 p.m., Sa. 10 a.m.-8 p.m., Su. 11 a.m.-7 p.m.

Want to get a load of the latest gadgets? Or to treat yourself to the newest iPhone as a souvenir? The Apple Store is your place to be.

11 WHOLE FOODS MARKET

238 Bedford Ave.

www.wholefoodsmarket.com

+1 718-734-2321

Mo.-Su. 8 a.m.-11 p.m.

Walking through Whole Foods is an experience in itself, but they also sell delectable takeout prepared meals. Then you'll be fully assimilated, because many New Yorkers don't cook.

12 JULIETTE

135 N 5th St.

www.juliettewilliamsburg.com

+1 718-388-9222

Su.-Th. 10:30 a.m.-11 p.m., Fr.-Sa. 10:30 a.m.-midnight

At Juliette you feel like you're in France. The chef prepares simple meals with the best ingredients in an attractive, nostalgic interior. In addition to French specialties such as onion soup *au gratin* and duck confit, the menu includes other dishes such as fries

and vegetable tagine, as well as a wide selection for vegetarians.

13 CAPRICES BY SOPHIE

138 N 6th St.

www.capricesbysophie.com

+1 347-689-4532

Mo.-Su. 8 a.m.-8 p.m.

It's impossible to walk into Caprices by Sophie without trying at least one *capricieux* – a fluffy meringue. The other cakes are delicious too. Relax for a while in the wonderful garden in the back.

14 BULLETIN

145 Wythe Ave.

www.bulletin-3.myshopify.com

+1 347-227-7790

Mo.-Sa. 11 a.m.-8 p.m., Su. 11 a.m.-7 p.m.

Need a t-shirt with a slogan like *Nasty Woman* or *The future is female*? A *Girl Power* necklace or a hoodie that says *goal digger*? Bulletin has them all and much more. Feminism is back!

15 CAFE MOGADOR

133 Wythe Ave.

www.cafemogador.com

+1 718-486-9222

Su.-Th. 9 a.m.-12:30 a.m., Fr.-Sa. 9 a.m.-1:30 a.m.

A restaurant serving Moroccan-inspired cuisine. Their 'Middle Eastern Eggs' brunch and 'Country

Breakfast' draw customers from all over the city. The locals' favorite for years.

EGG SHOP
109 N 3rd St., Williamsburg, Brooklyn
www.eggrestaurant.com
+1 718-302-5151
◷ Mo.-Fr. 7 a.m.-5 p.m.,
Sa.-Su. 8 a.m.-5 p.m.
The Egg Shop serves eggs in every form imaginable. *Vogue* called it 'The Egg-centric answer to your weekend brunch dilemma.' Let me not be the one to egg you on.

HEATONIST
121 Whythe Ave.
www.heatonist.com
+1 718-599-0838
◷ Mo.-Su. noon-8 p.m.
Hot sauce made from jalapeños grown on a New York rooftop? Check. Bottles covered in panthers and pumas? Check. So spicy you'll flood the city with your sweat? Possible. Tasting is allowed – if you dare.

ROUGH TRADE NYC
64 N 8th St.
www.roughtrade.com
+1 718-388-4111
◷ Mo.-Sa. 11 a.m.-11 p.m., Su. 11 a.m.-9 p.m.
This is the place to go if you're a vinyl fan. Sonos lets the music carry you away in comfort in the Listening Room.

BROOKLYN BOWL
61 Wythe Ave., Williamsburg, Brooklyn
www.brooklynbowl.com
+1 718 963 3369
◷ Sa. 11 a.m.-5 p.m., Su. 11 a.m.-6 p.m.
What better way to spend a family night out than a couple of hours' bowling? Enjoy yesteryear's hits, comfort food, and beer freshly brewed by the neighbors, Brooklyn Brewery. Sit comfortably in your Chesterfield while ogling the Williamsburg hipsters. Strike!

THE WILLIAM VALE
111 N 12th St., Williamsburg, Brooklyn
www.thewilliamvale.com
+1 718-631-8400
◷ Mo.-Th. 4 p.m.-midnight,
Fr. 4 p.m.-2 a.m., Sa. 2 p.m.-2 a.m.,
Su. 2 a.m.-midnight
This hotel's roof has the best view of New York. Unlike most places, the rooftop bar on the 22nd floor allows under-21s. You get a bird's-eye view of Brooklyn, Queens, and Manhattan. In the mood for a burger, fries, and ice cream? Head to Vale Park where you can enjoy a picnic on the grass thanks to Mister Dips, the cute vintage food truck.

LANGUAGES: <u>DUTCH, ENGLISH AND FRENCH</u>
FAVORITE VLOGGER: <u>CASEY NEISTAT</u>
FAVORITE ICE CREAM: <u>MORGENSTERN'S BLACK ICE CREAM</u>
HANGOUT: <u>LES COLEMAN SKATE PARK</u>
WANTS TO BE: <u>INFLUENCER/VLOGGER/TEACHER</u>
LIVES IN: <u>BELGIUM</u>

MATHIAS CRAZY SHAKES & IMPOSSIBLE BURGERS

The disadvantage of living away from my home country is that I don't see my family as often as I'd like. That certainly includes my nephew, Mathias, who's already 16. He comes to visit me once a year and then I try to make up for all that lost time. We go shopping in the hippest stores and try out the newest culinary trends. That's how we discovered the Japanese-inspired Mexican and the rainbow bagel. Great for wowing everybody on Instagram or Facebook.

As far as new food trends are concerned, Mathias is open to anything. One day we order a crazy milkshake at Black Tap and the next we have an impossible burger for lunch at Bareburger. The crazy shake is a real sugar bomb. Your milkshake's whipped cream is just a platform on which to build a tower of donuts or for layering a thick slice of Junior's cheesecake. This is then decorated with malt balls, chocolate bars, or other candy. But the impossible burger is actually very healthy. It's an organic burger made from meat substitutes, but you wouldn't know it from the taste. That's what's so great about New York. Everyone can find something to eat here, even the pickiest eaters.

During one of Mathias' visits we were taking a stroll on the High Line when he suddenly shouted: 'I know this!' It turned out that he recognized this part of the city from one of his computer games, *Grand Theft Auto*. There wasn't much about the High Line I could teach him; there wasn't a curve in the park, built on a raised train rail, that he didn't already know. But I did happen to know where the game's inventor lives. Dan Houser bought a shack in Brooklyn Heights for $12.5 million. So we went on to explore that neighborhood, because Houser was smart enough not to use his own neighborhood for the scenery.

Mathias' main hero is the vlogger and filmmaker Casey Neistat. I also follow him. With more than 8 million followers, he is one of the world's best-known, if not the best-known, vloggers. Ineke once bumped into him after a book presentation at Jack's Wife Freda, one of our favorite lunch places, which serves colorful dishes that are always an Instagram success. That evening, I had left a bit earlier. Shortly afterwards, Casey himself came on the scene and Ineke ended up in one of his vlogs. Every time I think about it I get jealous all over again... Fortunately, I walk around New York every day so chances are I'll still come across him somewhere. And if not, I'll just invite him to my next book presentation. Dream big; that's part of New York too.

A FEW TIPS FROM MATHIAS

LES COLEMAN SKATEPARK
62 Monroe St. and Pike St., Lower East Side
Sunrise to sunset.
newyorkcityskateparks.com
The skate plaza where you can literally jump over the Big Apple! Only the best skaters dare jump over the big red apple. This is the place to learn tricks from the experts.

MORGENSTERN'S FINEST ICE CREAM
2 Rivington St., between Bowery St. and Chrystie St., Little Italy
www.morgensternsnyc.com
+1 212-209-7684
Su.-Th. 8 a.m.-11 p.m., Fr.-Sa. 8 a.m.-midnight
Particularly famous for their black ice cream, but they also have a wide selection of other special flavors. Plan some extra time for your visit because they take their time decorating your ice cream to perfection with pretzels or cookies. But ice cream lovers like to watch.

FuN FACT
In 1884, 21 elephants crossed Brooklyn Bridge to convince the New Yorkers that it was strong enough.

A TIP FROM PATRICK

BAREBURGER
More than 10 locations in Manhattan.
www.bareburger.com
An organic restaurant offering delicious burgers and a children's menu that also has a lot to interest adults. If you need it, they'll give you a sippy cup, pencils for drawing, and last but certainly not least: the best fries in New York.
My favorite is the 'impossible burger.' It's vegetarian, but you can scarcely tell the difference.

START TO RUN?
Are 20,000 steps on your Fitbit not enough? Want to make sure you stay fit during your trip? Don't leave your running shoes at home. If you get up early for a jog on Brooklyn Bridge, it won't be crowded yet and the view is breathtaking. A lap in Central Park or a few in your hotel's swimming pool is also an option, of course.

THE STATUE OF LIBERTY

Liberty Island
www.statuecruises.com
If you want to see the Statue of Liberty for free, you can buy a return ticket for the Staten Island Ferry. If you want to go to Liberty Island, you need to buy tickets at Statue Cruises, which is only possible at Castle Clinton National Monument in Battery Park. Beware of swindlers trying to cheat you into buying phony tickets. To see Lady Liberty's crown, you need to make reservations a few months in advance. Children who want to visit the crown need to be at least 47 inches tall and capable of going up many stairs. Remember that this will be a day trip with a lot of waiting at the ferry.

FUN FACTS

The Statue of Liberty was a present from France to the United States in 1886 in honor of the Declaration of Independence's centennial and as a token of friendship. The statue was built by Gustave Eiffel, who also built the Eiffel Tower.

300 different hammers were used in the construction of the copper Statue of Liberty.

The Statue of Liberty was assembled in France and then shipped to New York in 214 crates. So in 1884 Lady Liberty was still in France.

When the Statue of Liberty first arrived from France it was copper-colored. It took about twenty years for it to become its current green-blue color.

'The Statue of Liberty' is actually a nickname. The actual name Bartholdi gave his gift was 'Liberty Enlightening the World'.

The seven points of the Statue of Liberty's crown symbolize the seven seas and the seven continents.

Every year, Lady Liberty is struck by lightning more than 600 times.

FAMOUS VLOGGERS

CASEY NEISTAT

Everyone knows that Casey Neistat is an American YouTube celebrity, filmmaker and vlogger. But did you also know that Casey Neistat grew up in Connecticut and left school at 16? Or that his first job was as a dishwasher in a fish restaurant? And that he moved to New York when he was 21 and worked as a bicycle messenger? He began vlogging in New York. He was the first to turn vlogging into an occupation by filming while rolling through the streets of New York on his skateboard.

He became one of the world's most famous vloggers and earns good bucks from it too, as evidenced by the trips he makes. He proposed to his wife Candice in Amsterdam, they got married in South Africa, and went on their honeymoon to Southeast Asia. They now also have a daughter, Francine (3). Casey was already a father. His son, Owen, is 19.

Also a big fan? Here are some places where you stand a chance of bumping into him:

CASEY NEISTAT'S OFFICE

368 Broadway, between White St. and Franklin St., Tribeca

www.casey.nyc

Stand outside his door with other die-hard fans and wait till Casey shows up on his skateboard.

BLACK TAP

529 Broome St., between Sullivan St. and Thompson St., SoHo

136 W 55th St., between 6th and 7th Ave., Midtown

www.blacktapnyc.com

Su.-We. 11 a.m.-midnight, Th.-Sa. 11 a.m.-1 a.m.

These shakes and burgers don't dominate social media for no reason. They look stunning and also have a stunning amount of calories. Maybe not such a bad idea to share one. When stars like Casey come here for a burger or a shake it usually affects the length of the line.

JACK'S WIFE FREDA

50 Carmine St., between Bedford St. and Bleecker St., West Village

224 Lafayette St., between Broome St. and Spring St., SoHo

www.jackswifefreda.com

Mo.-Sa. 8:30 a.m.-midnight, Su. 8:30 a.m.-10 p.m.

A popular and friendly little restaurant that serves the best waffles (Lafayette St.) and the best pancakes (Carmine St.). But they have something for every hour of the day: delicious sandwiches, lasagna with lamb and eggplant, spicy chicken, or crunchy schnitzels. Very child-friendly and cozy too.

SARA DIETSCHY

This YouTube vlogger (born in 1994) is best-known for her web series, Creative Spaces TV, in which she profiles a variety of artists and sheds light on their working methods. Her most renowned clip, with almost 2 million views, is *How to Casey Neistat a vlog*. Sara has been living in New York since 2017. She likes discovering the city together with her boyfriend, skateboarder and YouTuber, John Hill.

Here are some places you're likely to bump into Sara Dietschy:

CHELSEA PIERS SKATE PARK
Pier 62, 143 11th Ave., Chelsea
www.hudsonriverpark.org
+1 212-242-6427
Mo.-Su. 8 a.m.-8 p.m.

Sara often hangs out with her boyfriend, John Hill, in New York's skate parks. If you like roller skating, you'll like Chelsea Piers. Let yourself go on (get ready for some skating terms…) the Ollie Ledge, the Kinked Flat Rail, Wedge, Intermediate Fun Box… It's easy to get there by crossing the street at West 22nd St. in Chelsea. Don't forget your helmet–it's compulsory. Other protective gear is advisable, of course.

IRVING FARM
71 Irving Pl., between E 18th St. and E 19th St., Gramercy
And seven other locations in Manhattan
www.irvingfarm.com
+1 212-995-5252
Mo.-Fr. 7 a.m.-8 p.m., Sa.-Su. 8 a.m.-8 p.m.

Irving Farm started in 1996 when two friends opened a coffee house in Gramercy Park. Shortly thereafter they started roasting coffee in Dutchess County. Now Irving Farm has become a household name, with eight branches in Manhattan. A definite must for coffee lovers or Sara Dietschy fans.

SWEETGREEN
W 42nd St., between 5th and 6th Aves., Midtown
And twenty other locations in New York
www.sweetgreen.com
+1 917-993-5070
Mo.-Fr. 10:30 a.m.-10 p.m., Sa.-Su. 10:30 a.m.-6 p.m.

Sweetgreen serves healthy salads made using vegetables bought from small and mid-sized growers. You can create your own salad or choose ingredients from the suggestions. Without a doubt, the best salads in New York.

THE SOUVENIR HUNTER

FOR STUFFED ANIMAL LOVERS

PICCOLINI NYC
167 Mott St., between Broome St. and
Grand St., Little Italy
www.piccolininyc.com
+1 212-775-1118
Mo.-Sa. 11 a.m.-7 p.m.
Piccolini NYC's owner designs romp-
ers and t-shirts adorned with images of
pretzels and hotdogs for the small-size
New Yorkers. Super cute. Marie likes to
buy presents for her friends there.

HAZEL VILLAGE
510 3rd Ave., between 11th St. and 12th St.,
Park Slope, Brooklyn
www.hazelvillage.com
+1 929-237-6941
Mo.-Sa. 10 a.m.-7 p.m., Su. 10 a.m.-5 p.m.
These cute stuffed animals have the
most beautiful clothes and are also
available in larger sizes (up to 5 years).
Who wouldn't want to 'twin' (wear the
same outfit) with their cuddly toy?

A TIP FROM MARIE

Check out their activities. They
offer neat crafting classes where
you can have your toy personalized
with a monogram, such as
your initials.

FOR TREASURE HUNTERS

CHINATOWN
Canal St., between Bowery St. and Mulberry St., Chinatown
The shops here sell everything. From *I love
New York* t-shirts to key chains and magnets.
They also have the latest fads, such as fidget
spinners. You won't believe the treasures you'll
find here for just a couple of dollars.

FOR 'HARDCORE' NEW YORK LOVERS

HARDROCK CAFE
1501 Broadway, Times Square
www.hardrock.com
+1 212-343-3355
Mo.-Su. 8 a.m.-1 a.m.
Hard Rock Cafe fan? Then your closet calls for a
Hard Rock Cafe New York hoodie!

SOAP CHERIE
218 Bedford Ave. and North Fifth St., Williamsburg, Brooklyn
www.soapcherie.com
+1 718-388-1165
Mo.-Fr. 10:30 a.m.-20:30 p.m., Sa.-Su. 10:30 a.m.-9 p.m.
If you still want to smell like New York once
you're back home, then here's the place to buy
charcoal or mud soap. Or do you prefer the unicorn cupcake soap? No problem.

CANNED AIR FROM NEW YORK CITY

The air in New York is like nowhere else in the world. For those who can't get enough of it, Canned Air From (on www.etsy.com) have now canned it. These tin cans lower stress, cure homesickness, and are good cures for nostalgia.

Every year more than 61 million tourists come to New York City. That sure is a lot of souvenirs...

GROWN-UPS ONLY

NY DISTILLERY DOROTHY PARKER GIN
79 Richardson St., between Lorimer St. and Leonard St., Williamsburg, Brooklyn
www.nydistilling.com
+1 718-412-0874
Mo. 6 p.m.-midnight, Tu.-Th. 6 p.m.-2 a.m., Fr. 5 p.m.-2 a.m., Sa.-Su. 2 p.m.-midnight
Take a tour of the distillery on weekends and enjoy a taster at the Shanty bar next to the distillery.

DEVOCIÓN
69 Grand St., between Kent Ave. and Barc Ave., Williamsburg, Brooklyn
www.devocion.com
+1 718-285-6180
Mo.-Fr. 7 a.m.-7 p.m., Sa.-Su. 8 a.m.-7 p.m.
NY Daily News describes Devoción as a 'killer cup of coffee.' Why not drop by and take a look at how they roast their beans? Taste the different types of coffee and take home a bag of your favorite beans. Great for aromatizing your suitcase...

THE NO
TIMES
IS THE
OF HO

SE OF

QUARE

SOUND

E

HENRI

HANGOUT: <u>SOHO</u>
FAVORITE PLACE: <u>ASPHALT GREEN FOR PLAYING SOCCER</u>
FAVORITE SNACK: <u>BAGEL AT RUSS & DAUGHTERS</u>
WANTS TO BE: <u>ARCHITECT</u>
FAVORITE BUILDING IN NY: <u>FREEDOM TOWER</u>
LANGUAGES: <u>ENGLISH, DUTCH, AND SPANISH</u>
HOBBIES: <u>SOCCER, DRAWING, GUITAR, CHESS, HANGING OUT WITH FRIENDS</u>
FAVORITE ICE CREAM: <u>BEN & JERRY'S MILK AND COOKIES</u>
LIVES IN: <u>LOWER EAST SIDE</u>

HENRI THE SOUND OF HOME

One day I was walking in Midtown Manhattan when I saw a young guy race by on his skateboard. Only later did I realize it was Henri, the son of my good friends, Philip and Esther. I got to know him when he was still a toddler but now he's a 15-year-old teenager. He taught me what New York teenagers like to do most. From an afternoon of soccer on Asphalt Green to a U2 concert in Madison Square Garden. Getting bored is not an option when you grow up in New York.

Henri's favorite way of spending the day is going to a sports game in Madison Square Garden. Although it's actually the New York fans who make it an unforgettable experience. After a game in which the Knicks only just beat the Bulls, the cheering was so loud that the ear-splitting noise made it impossible to have a conversation for a couple of hours.

Henri's favorite neighborhood for hanging out is SoHo, with the Supreme Store as his favorite shop. Every Thursday they bring in new clothes. Even if new means that one of their logo's letters has a new color, every Thursday there are long wait lines at the door. The lines are controlled to keep them from blocking traffic. Just like in amusement parks, zigzag lines are organized, supervised by a burly, intimidating security guard. Actually, most of the people in the line don't even know what's new that day, but they don't care. Anything Supreme produces is hip. Henri doesn't mind standing in line for three hours for the newest hoodie or beanie. Some of those collectors' items also sell well online. I sometimes see them on eBay with staggeringly high price tags, sometimes as high as $10,000. That's why many clients bring their own bags to carry home their new purchases. Just imagine your brand new Supreme hoodie being stolen in the subway...

Henri wouldn't want to live anywhere else but New York. It's a city that's always abuzz, where you can always find something new, and where you can taste the cuisine of the whole world. He likes sleeping over with a friend who lives right next to Times Square, and they sleep with the window open. For Henri, the fire engine sirens and the cabs' beeping horns are the sound of home. That's the hallmark of a true New Yorker.

☰ A FEW TIPS FROM HENRI

SUPREME

274 Lafayette St. and Prince St., NoLIta
152 Grand St., between Berry St. and Bedford
Ave., Greenpoint, Brooklyn
www.supremenewyork.com
Mo.-Sa. 11 a.m.-6 p.m., Su. noon-6 p.m.
Want the just-arrived t-shirt or the
hoodie? Take your place in line.

ASPHALT GREEN

212 North End Ave., between Warren St. and
Murray St., Battery Park City
Mo.-Fr. 5:30 a.m.-10:30 p.m., Sa.-Su. 7 a.m.-8 p.m.
555, E 90th St., Upper East Side
Mo.-Fr. 5:30 a.m.-10 p.m., Sa.-Su. 8 a.m.-8 p.m.
www.asphaltgreen.org
Want to play some soccer on one of the
nicest fields in New York City? Then
head to Asphalt Green, the soccer
fans' favorite spot.

BEN & JERRY'S

30 Rockefeller Center, W 49th St., between
5th and 6th Aves., Midtown
Mo.-Su. 10 a.m.-11 p.m.
200 W 44th St., between 7th and 8th Aves.,
Times Square
Su.-Th. 11 a.m.-midnight, Fr.-Sa. 11 a.m.-1 a.m.
www.benjerry.com
Who can say no to a scoop of
Cherry Garcia or Stephen Colbert's
American Dream?

FUN FACT

Ben & Jerry's creators, Ben Cohen & Jerry
Greenfield, got to know each other in gym class
in Long Island when they were 14. They were
the slowest in the class but became pretty fast
businessmen.

NUMBER ONE BAGELS

Never confuse a bagel with a donut. Admittedly, they both have a hole, but that's where the similarity ends. A bagel is less sweet and less greasy than a donut and can be spread with anything you like. A typical New York bagel is topped with cream cheese, smoked salmon, and onion. The Polish immigrants brought the bagel to the United States. In the old days, most shops were closed on Sundays but you could always get challah (a braided bread) or bagels in the Jewish quarter. Pretty soon, the Jewish bakers were riding around the city with bread wagons.

Bagels are often sprinkled with poppy or sesame seeds, but most New Yorkers like their bagels plain, with no frills. Great for breakfast, lunch, or a snack and ideal as travel food.

FUN FACT

In the 17th century the bagel was considered the best present you could give to a woman who had just given birth. Ideal for regaining your strength.

RUSS & DAUGHTERS

The Shop: 179 E Houston St., between Allan St. and Orchard St., NoLIta
The Cafe: 127 Orchard St., between Delancey St. and Rivington St., NoLIta
At the Jewish museum, 1109 5th Ave., between E 92nd and E 93rd St., Upper East Side
+1 212-475-4880
www.shop.russanddaughters.com
Mo.-We. 8 a.m.-6 p.m., Th. 8 a.m.-7 p.m., Fr.-Su. 8 a.m.-6 p.m.

Without a doubt, the best bagels in New York City! Choose from different types of cream and salmon. But New Yorkers also come to Russ & Daughters especially for the chocolate babka.

THE BAGEL STORE

754 Metropolitan Ave. and Graham Ave., Williamsburg, Brooklyn (closing down in 2019)
69 5th Ave., between Warren St. and St Mark's Pl., Park Slope, Brooklyn
www.thebagelstore.com
+1 718-782-5856
Mo.-Su. 7 a.m.-6 p.m.

Scott Rossillo calls himself the first bagel artist. He also invented the original rainbow bagel, and he sells cragels. These are the offspring of the croissant and the bagel.

MUSIC IN NEW YORK

Dreaming of becoming famous? Start by making your first videos here in New York and putting them on your own YouTube channel. The skyline is always impressive; it's also how Justin Bieber got started. Times Square has green boxes painted on the ground where you should stand if you want to sing a song between Mickey Mouse and Spider-Man.

If you want to sing in the subway, you have to audition first, because you need a permit. Who needs Carnegie Hall when you can play on Union Square 14th Street?

MUSIC IN CENTRAL PARK

BREAKDANCE RAPPERS

In the Mall, across from Bethesda Fountain, you'll often find a show involving six or so burly men performing feats. Really fun to watch. Until they pick eight men out of the crowd to jump over. It'll cost you $20 to avoid this dangerous stunt... so choose your spot wisely. The motto is: 'be inconspicuous.'

JOHN LENNON

Strawberry Fields was created to commemorate John Lennon. This teardrop-shaped section of the park also includes the Imagine Sign, a beautiful round mosaic. Beatles fans are always here, paying tribute to their idols.

In 1984, Yoko Ono gave a $500,000 grant to Central Park for the renovation and maintenance of Strawberry Fields.

FUN FACT

Yoko Ono didn't want a statue of her husband, so that his head would not be soiled by pigeons.

GLOBAL CITIZEN FESTIVAL
www.globalcitizen.org

A big charity concert has been held every September since 2011 on the Great Lawn, a large closely-mown field. The proceeds amount to $35 million (!). Every year, stars such as Stevie Wonder, Beyoncé, and Coldplay perform here. Tickets are free but you have to earn them by performing many acts of charity.

MUSIC IN THE CITY

ROUGH TRADE
64 N 8th St., Williamsburg, Brooklyn
www.roughtrade.com
+1 718-388-4111
Mo.-Sa. 11 a.m.-11 p.m., Su. 11 a.m.-9 p.m.
Do you like browsing through vinyl records? Then this is the place for you. Sonos allows you to enjoy the ultimate audio experience in the Listening Room.

APOLLO THEATER
253 W 125th St., Harlem
www.apollotheater.org
+1 212-531-5300
Amateur Night at the Apollo Theater is world famous. Stars such as Ella Fitzgerald, Billie Holiday, Mariah Carey, and The Jackson Five were discovered here.

The cool thing about Amateur Night is that the public helps decide who gets pulled off the stage and who can stay. Who knows? You might just happen to be there when the new Michael Jackson is discovered.

GRAFFITI

THE BUSHWICK COLLECTIVE
St Nicholas Ave. and Troutman St.
www.thebushwickcollective.com
If you take the L train to the Jefferson stop, you get out into New York's graffiti mecca. This is thanks to The Bushwick Collective. This artists' collective, led by Joe Ficalora, has breathed new life into the neighborhood. Admire all the impressive, and often also amusing, works of art painted on what used to be dull walls.

A TIP FROM INEKE
Take a closer look at Lola Grass' work. This seven-year-old 'bad ass' is the youngest graffiti artist in the world. As well as on the wall at The Bushwick Collective, her work can be seen on Coney Island and at Art Basel in Wynwood, Miami.

A TIP FROM PATRICK
My fellow guide, Tim Marschang from Antwerp, gives graffiti tours. That's how the idea arose of starting a website, and now an app too, to showcase all the coolest graffiti. Want to know where you can admire the best pieces? Check www.streetartcities.com or download the app: Street Art Cities.

LANGUAGES: ENGLISH, FRENCH, AND SPANISH
HOBBIES: PAINTING WITH HER DOG, MR. BIG, PEOPLE-WATCHING ON THE STREETS OF NEW YORK, GOING OUT TO ALL THE CLUBS
FAVORITE RESTAURANTS: XYST AND BY CHLOE
WEBSITE: WWW.ADELINEART.COM
INSTAGRAM: @ADELINEART_
LIVES IN: HARLEM, MANHATTAN

ADELINE SAVE THE PLANET

Like many other hopefuls in New York, I also started in the food sector. Businessman Yves Jadot gave me my first job in his Belgian restaurant, Petit Abeille. The American dream? Yves knows all about it. He built a whole empire of restaurants and bars from scratch. He has always been an inspiration to me. When I worked in Petit Abeille, I got to know his children, Adeline and Pascal. I watched them grow up and mature into fine adults. Their successful father could have helped them start a business career but they preferred to make their own choices. I can't help but admire that.

I sometimes worry that my daughter Marie won't have the same opportunities as her male peers but, thanks to Adeline (21), I know I shouldn't have to. She goes her own way, not caring what others may think. Adeline is a promising artist. She studied art at Boulder University. To make a little something on the side and to perfect her painting techniques, she makes paintings and sells them to restaurants. Through her art, Adeline wants to encourage people to contemplate their fixed patterns of thought. The American daughter of a Belgian father and a Jamaican mother who grew up in New York, she knows all too well how passé pigeon-holing is.

Her brother, Pascal, is studying piano at the Brussels Conservatory. On one of his home visits he convinced the whole family to switch to eating vegan.

Yves saw right away that it wasn't a whim and that his son wasn't the only one who realized that the planet would be better off if we didn't consume meat and animal products on such a large scale. This led him to include vegan dishes on all his restaurants' menus. He was heaped with praise for it. He has even opened a vegan restaurant, XYST, for vegan lovers as well as for the love of his children. Adeline created the paintings for this restaurant too: a man with a cow's head and a woman with a pig's head. 'Would you still eat me if I wore a dress?' is the inscription. A fitting tongue-in-cheek message for this restaurant.

The secret to success in New York? Take a look at the Jadots and you'll come to a few conclusions. Follow your passion, dare to adapt, be flexible in a constantly changing city, and work hard. That'll get you far. By the way, failure is not a disgrace in New York. No one is ashamed of going out of business. To quote the Irish writer, Samuel Beckett: 'Fail, fail more, fail better.' Anyone with the courage to take risks has failed at one time or another. But it teaches you a lot. Just try again and, hopefully, you'll be more successful. That's the New York spirit.

TIE YOUR LACES
TO YOUR LINE

I ♥ NY

NYC SUBWAY
INSPIRED LACES

📧 A FEW TIPS FROM PATRICK

ALL BIRDS SOHO
68 Prince St., between Crosby St.
and Lafayette St., SoHo
www.allbirds.com
+1 888-963-8944
Mo.-Su. 10 a.m.-8 p.m.
This is the store for sneakers made
from fine merino wool with insoles
containing castor bean oil. The sneakers are washable and don't carry a
logo. Their mission was to create a
stylish shoe made from sustainable
materials. Accomplished. Marie and
I twin (we both wear the same shoes),
but Emma Watson is also a fan.

FUN FACT

Year after year, the animal rights
organization, PETA, declares New York one of
the most vegan-friendly cities in the world.

XYST
44 W 17th St., between 5th and 6th Aves.
www.matthewkenneycuisine.com
+1 212-727-2979
Mo.-Su. 5 p.m.-11 p.m.
Yves Jadot's newest restaurant and already the
talk of the town. If you're vegan, you have to try
this for a special occasion–it's quite chic. I can't
wait to take Ineke here.

📧 A TIP FROM ADELINE

DIA: BEACON
3 Beekman St., Beacon
www.diaart.org
+1 845-440-0100
Jan. to March: Fr.-Mo. 11 a.m.-4 p.m., April to Oct.:
Fr.-Mo. 11 a.m.-6 p.m., Nov. to Dec.: Th.-Mo. 11 a.m.-4 p.m.
Dia: Beacon is in Upstate New York, a one-hour-
and-twenty-minute train ride from Grand
Central. This used to be where the Nabisco (of
Oreo fame) Company's boxes were printed.
Today it's one of the largest open-air modern
art museums. It's a great park for relaxation and
inspiration.

GLUTEN-FREE & VEGAN FAVORITES

ERIN MCKENNA'S BAKERY
248 Broome St., Lower East Side
www.erinmckennasbakery.com
+1 855-462-2292
Su.-Mo. 10 a.m.-8 p.m., Tu.-Th. 10 a.m.-10 p.m., Fr.-Su. 10 a.m.-11 p.m.
The pastries sold here are entirely gluten-free, vegan, and contain no refined sugars, milk, soy, eggs, or wheat. Sounds boring but these cupcakes, donuts, and éclairs are big in New York, and have been so even since before gluten-free became so trendy.

THE LITTLE BEET TABLE
333 Park Ave. S, between E 24th St. and E 25th St., Flatiron District
www.thelittlebeettable.com
+1 212-466-3330
Mo.-Th. 11:30 a.m.-10 p.m., Fr. 11:30 a.m.-10:30 p.m., Sa. 10 a.m.-10:30 p.m., Su. 10 a.m.-9 p.m.
A restaurant serving healthy food in a modern and homey setting. Vegetables are paramount but non-vegetarian dishes are also available, and gluten-free is not a problem.

BY CHLOE
185 Bleecker St. and Macdougal St., SoHo
And six other locations in New York
www.eatbychloe.com
+1 212-290-8000
Mo.-Fr. 11 a.m.-11 p.m., Sa.-Su. 10 a.m.-11 p.m.
As a vegan, you know you're in the right place if the slogan is 'Eat well, dream big and keep it vegan!' By Chloe is the thing for New York vegans.

BEYOND SUSHI
229 E 14th St., between 2nd and 3rd Aves., Union Square
And four other locations in Manhattan
www.beyondsushinyc.com
+1 646-861-2889
Mo.-Su. 11:30 a.m.-9:30 p.m.
Ever tasted vegan sushi? This is your big chance! Beyond Sushi's menu is 100% vegan. On top of that, all their restaurants are child-friendly. So it's no problem for the owners to bring their own children along.

BETWEEN YOUNGSTER AND ADULT

FAKE ID

You can drive a car in America from the age of 16 but you have to be 21 to legally drink alcohol. Teenagers have a creative solution for that. They simply order a fake ID on the internet. It's not without risk; the penalties are severe. You could get a year in jail or 3 years suspended with a $1000 fine. And as if that weren't bad enough, you would then have a criminal record, which could make finding an internship or a job very difficult. Still, most teenagers can't resist.

A TIP FROM PATRICK

Being a tourist doesn't stop you from renting a car, although New York traffic can be chaotic, to put it mildly. If you're still up to the challenge, it's best to arrange an international driver's license in advance. If you stay in the US longer than 3 months, you have to take another test.

SEE MORE ON
BE**NY**
Minute
/BENYMINUTE

≣ A TIP FROM PATRICK

WESTLIGHT WILLIAM VALE
111 N 12th St., Williamsburg, Brooklyn
www.westlightnyc.com
+1 718-307-7100
Mo.-Th. 4 p.m.-midnight, Fr. 4 p.m.-2 a.m., Sa. 2 p.m.-2 a.m., Su. 2 p.m.-midnight

This rooftop bar can't be beat for its amazing view of the Manhattan skyline, Brooklyn, and Queens. To top it off, you can get in even if you're under 21 and wearing sneakers.

TATTOO PARLORS

In New York getting a tattoo is legal from the age of 18. At a hip cocktail bar I recently saw a man with an avocado tattoo. When I asked him why he said he simply likes avocados. Tattoos are nothing out of the ordinary in New York; even a bit banal.
Tattoos aren't cheap either. Check beforehand that the parlor is reliable if you don't want to end up with the wrong inscription.

FuN FAcT

Tattooing was forbidden in New York between 1961 and 1997, following an outbreak of Hepatitis B. Of course this didn't mean nobody got tattoos; they just happened underground.

BANG BANG

328 Broome St., between Bowery St. and Chrysthie St., Lower East Side
www.bangbangforever.com
+1 212-219-2799
Mo.-Fr. 11 a.m.-11 p.m.
Keith McCurdy, otherwise known as Bang Bang, has tattooed the likes of Adele, Katy Perry, Rihanna, and Justin Bieber. His trademark is tattoos in somber black and shades of gray. Check out his Instagram page (@bangbangnyc), where you'll also see the fantastic tattoo artists with whom he collaborates.

RIVINGTON TATTOO NYC

175 Rivington St., between Clinton St. and Attorney St., Lower East Side
www.rivingtontattoo.com
+1 212-256-0281
Mo.-Th. noon-8 p.m., Fr.-Sa. noon-9 p.m., Su. noon-6 p.m.
There's a cool vibe in this tattoo parlor. It's where tattoo artists Ethan Morgan, Jim White, and Olivia do their thing. Vloggers such as the Dutch Claire Lucia love getting tattooed here.

NYC SKYSCRAPER FACTS

CHRYSLER BUILDING

- Height: 1046 feet
- Stories: 77
- Built in: 1928
- Fun fact: It was the tallest building in the world for 11 months before it was surpassed by the Empire State Building

FLATIRON BUILDING

- Height: 285 feet
- Stories: 22
- Built in: 1902
- Fun fact: When it was opened, The New York Times called it a monstrosity. Now it is considered one of New York's most beautiful buildings

30 ROCKEFELLER PLAZA, TOP OF THE ROCK

- Height: 850 feet
- Stories: 70
- Built in: 1933
- Fun fact: There are 1215 stairs to reach the top; alternately, the elevator will get you there in 42 seconds

EMPIRE STATE BUILDING

- Height: 1454 feet
- Stories: 102
- Built in: 1930
- Fun fact: built in 410 days

ONE WORLD TRADE CENTER

- Height: 1776 feet
- Stories: 104
- Built in: 2006
- Fun fact: 1776 feet tall, same as the year of America's independence

WOOLWORTH BUILDING

- Height: 792 feet
- Stories: 58
- Built in: 1913
- Fun fact: Mr. Woolworth paid for the building in cash (13 million dollars)

NYC SUBWAY

FuN FACTs

There are 472 subway stops in New York City. That's more than in any other metropolis.

During the 2016 presidential elections, both Hillary Clinton and Bernie Saunders wanted to show that they were ordinary people who take the subway. But they both bombed: it took Hillary Clinton five swipes with her subway card before she managed to get through and Bernie Saunders thought he could still pay with tokens even though they were discontinued way back in 2003.

In 1993, 16-year-old subway freak, Keron Thomas, steered an A train for 3.5 hours before he got caught. The judge was so impressed with this feat that he imposed only a suspended 3-year sentence.

Anyone wanting to play music in the subway first has to audition at the MTA (Metropolitan Transportation Authority). So it's not just any old musicians you hear in the subway.

On August 7, 2013 an 18-inch shark took the N train. No one knows how the shark got into the subway and the case wasn't investigated. Theories vary from an escaped Chinatown shark to a Discovery Channel publicity stunt, since it happened to be their Shark Week at the time. Unfortunately the fish didn't survive the journey.

The price for a slice of pizza is always the same as for a one-way subway ticket (now $2.75). So when the price of a subway ride goes up, so does the price of a pizza slice.

When old subway cars are retired they are thrown into the Atlantic, where they get appropriated by animals and plants. An idea of how this may look can be seen in the Houston Street station, with *Platform Diving*, an artwork by Deborah Brown.

VINTAGE-CHIC

New York is the largest city in the world's most polluting country. Every month, Americans produce about as much garbage as they weigh. One way to combat this and at the same time be the most original dresser is to check out the vintage shops. Sometimes you'll have look for quite a while but there are great finds to be had for next to nothing. The chances that you'll meet someone at a party dressed the same are as good as non-existent.

BEACON'S CLOSET

74 Guernsey St., between Norman Ave. and Nassay Ave., Williamsburg, Brooklyn
www.beaconscloset.com
+1 718-486-0816
Mo.-Su. 11 a.m.-8 p.m.

The way to have a real New Yorker's aroma lingering on your clothing is to browse through the racks at Beacon's Closet.

L TRAIN VINTAGE

204 1st Ave., between 12th St. and 13th St., East Village
And five other locations in New York .
ltrainvintage.com
+1 212-228-5201
Su.-Th. noon-8 p.m., Fr.-Sa. noon-9 p.m.

If you're looking for a unique item of clothing, you will definitely find it here. A unique Tommy Hilfiger jacket from the 80s, jean jackets with your favorite cartoon characters embroidered on them, or sneakers that are no longer available? You can get them all at L Train Vintage.

At the beginning of the 19th century, garbage disposal in New York consisted mainly of pigs that roamed the streets in search of food.

Subject index

Photo credits

More insider tips and tricks about New York City in the bestseller *BE NY – From Tourist to New Yorker*
ISBN 9 789401434690

- *BE NY – From Tourist to New Yorker* is an original city guide, which will lead you quickly and easily through the Big Apple.
- Where can you find the best spots to enjoy art, culture or good food? How do you shop economically and which shops are a must?
- Find new hot spots and the coolest places in New York with the tips from Patrick van Rosendaal and 22 colorful New Yorkers.
- Discover the different New York neighborhoods on foot, by boat or by bike, using carefully mapped-out routes.
- On the way, be entertained by many fun facts and interesting anecdotes.

'Living in the land of the free, I've found the definitive guide to the world's most bustling metropolis. Patrick van Rosendaal is a splendid storyteller. He knows every nook and cranny. He is Mr. New York City.'

BJÖRN SOENENS, US Correspondent for Belgian VRT NWS

WWW.LANNOO.COM

Big thank you to the BE NY family

THE YOUNGEST MEMBER OF OUR FAMILY:

Our very own little New Yorker, Marie! Thank you for your inspiration, motivation, and boundless energy. If you've had to eat too many ice creams, I'm sorry. If in the future you say that you always had to try out new playgrounds, even when you occasionally would have rather stayed home, we won't dispute it. But you know that we always did it out of love. Without you we never would have embarked on this book.

Also, many thanks to The Learning Experience team, in particular to Marie's teachers, Miss Melina, Miss Mary and Principal Nicole. Your loving care gave us the time to do research and to write.

BE NY FAMILY FRIENDS:

Marie's friends and all her fans and admirers (great-grandma Mariëtte, grandma Mieke, granddad, grandma, Peter, Mathias, Arle, Uncle Paul...).
And of course, our mini-guides in particular: Elliot, Max, Markus, Marie, Blue, Lily, Evie, Roman, Leonie, Felice, Shira, Manon, Frasier, Mathias, Henri, Adeline, and their parents, brothers, sisters, and owners. Thanks also to the many friends, relatives, and clients for their involvement, good tips, and for being our guinea pigs. A special mention to Ilajah and his mother, Sarah, for the fantastic title.
A special thank you to our friends Björn and Emma for all their support, cozy dinners, and inspiring conversations.

BE NY FAMILY COMMUNITY:

Our ever-expanding community of NY lovers. Loyal customers, Facebook friends, Instagram followers, YouTube followers, and readers... You give us the energy to go out there every day and search for the best places. Also a big thank you to the many coffee houses that served as offices, such as A/D/C, Bluestone Lane, Communitea, Odd Fox Coffee, and in particular Indie

(43-10 Crescent St., LIC, Queens). Your pastries helped us get through when things got tough.

All the BE NY guides, especially Will van Mossevelde. Will, we're convinced you'll break through on Broadway and hereby reserve front row seats. Also thanks to the other city guides, our colleagues from GANYC for their constructive engagement and tips: you guys are great! Thanks to the Upper East Side moms, especially to dog-lover Liz Guize Bresler.

BE NY FAMILY PARTNERS:

Co-author Maaike Floor: you always found the words we were looking for to convey our enthusiasm about New York to our customers.

Photographer Robert Caplin: with every photo-shoot you surprise us anew with your talent, dedication, and unlimited patience.

Duval Branding Team: Marc Wellens, partner from the outset, André Duval and Kelly Vanhooreweder, Griet Ghys, Lieze Stevens, Dirk Zwaneveld.

You are our creative family. We're proud to be able to collaborate with you.

Ronny Bayens: your charisma, warm heart, and shared passion for New York are a constant source of inspiration. Your Connections Team feels like family, for which we are grateful.

Plantoys: we can't imagine better toys for Marie and her friends.

Christian Loos of KitchenNY: thank you for your creative inspiration and for all your support. You are a brother from another mother.

Lieven Defour, Hilde Snauwaert, and Anne Haegeman of Lannoo: thank you for your support and trust. Good news! We already have a proposal for book #4.

We love our family! Thank you!

Patrick and Ineke

WHO IS MAAIKE?

From her very first time in New York, Maaike knew she
was in the city's clutches. Most metropolises have a
couple of lively neighborhoods where life never stops.
In New York this is true of most of the neighborhoods and
you can think of the subway system as veins, pumping
blood to the whole body.

Thanks to Patrick, Maaike got to know New York's more
obscure aspects, such as Night Court, hidden restaurants,
and a night cafe that bears a suspicious resemblance to
a drug store. They share a love of telling stories. Maaike
also explored the city with Ineke and Marie and thus in-
creased their enthusiasm for working on this book.

At the beginning of 2000 Maaike worked for a while as
a journalist for the Amsterdam newspaper *Het Parool*.
Since 2003, she has been working for the *Gazet* in
Antwerp. As well as Antwerp, she has reported from
America, India, Bangladesh, the Philippines, Russia,
Greece, France, Finland, Croatia, and Italy. Maaike lives
in Antwerp with her husband and two sons (ages 3 and 7).
They like taking city and nature trips together. Her ultimate dream? A house in the Ardennes and an apartment
in New York. Although co-writing this book was also a
dream come true.